序　言

—— 沒有人天生就精通秘書的十八般武藝，什麼專業知識都需要學習，*English For Secretaries* 這本書處處為您設想，讓您在短期內把握住秘書英語的要訣，在職業競技場上，穩操勝算。

＊ 由淺入深，舉例最詳盡，資料最豐富 ＊

本書從「秘書英語入門」開始，翔實介紹秘書這一行的現況與出路，並且以圖解的方式，分條列出秘書的職務、工作範圍、秉性與能力，讓您開門見山，豁然開朗，瞭解到秘書身負的職責攸關重大，的確不可小覷。

「秘書英語必備常識」這一章，揭露秘書必須精通的諸種範疇，舉凡英語書信的視覺技巧、書寫信函的原則以及書信的新規則、新格式，都有詳細完整的介紹，讓您不致與潮流的歸趨脫節，掌握時代的訊息。

其次，「秘書求職與面談」，教您如何找到求職的門路，面試的事前準備要項、服裝儀容與評分標準等，均闢有專文解說，並附有「秘書面談實例」作為參考，讓您無往而不利。

＊ 本書幫您步上專業秘書的坦途 ＊

「包羅最廣泛」是本書最大的特色。「模範秘書英語書信」、「秘書電話英語」、「國際禮儀電報」等各章，一一呈現寫好

英文書信、電報與精通電話英語的秘訣。以鉅細靡遺，循序漸進的內容，清晰美觀的編排，讓您立即收到舉一反三，融會貫通的效果。

如何和客戶應對、翻譯，也是 *English For Secretaries* 的重點之一。「秘書接待英語」、「秘書翻譯對策」這兩章卽針對此，務期讓您在應對態度、接待英語、翻譯技巧與原則等各方面，均能拿捏得恰如其分。

本章每一章均附有「秘書自我測驗」，並特闢「秘書必備常識」，從秘書服裝，宴會的飲酒常識，介紹的先後順序，到安排商業午餐，名片的收受，White Tie 與 Black Tie 的區別，均有詳細的文字介紹，讓您在各種場合，永遠表現合宜、出色，深獲上司倚重。

成熟、有智慧的您，讀了本書，將步向專業秘書的坦途，迎向愉快、充滿自信的未來。

編者　謹識

目錄

第1章

秘書英語入門

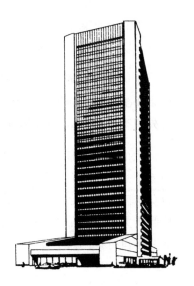

磨鍊國際性辨識力

由於交通工具及通訊技術的日新月異，使得國際間互動關係愈形複雜。世界變小了，他國發生的事件，馬上就直接影響到我們的國家及企業。居於公司要職的人，必須快速處理大量的資訊並期適時正確的下達判斷，才算克盡職責。隨時湧進的資訊，使得他們來不及一一處置，而必須找一個處理瑣事和資料的人，這個必須兼有**高度知識、常識**以輔佐上司的人就是秘書。

秘書是年輕女性夢寐以求的職業，能流利使用英文的**雙語秘書**（*bilingual secretary*）更是職業婦女的夢想。因此，在外國機構，大使館及外商公司，負責輔佐上司的秘書職業，便充滿了無限的吸引力。

其實雙語秘書，並不只是在外商公司才需要，台灣大部分的貿易公司以及中小企業，也有大量需求，因為台灣的經濟活動無不與各國的出入口交易或技術合作息息相關。

況且國內企業國際化程度年年提高，每年出國的人數也有顯著的遞增。無論是大型企業或者小公司，用**外語**（尤其是英文）收發信件，接待外國客戶，打電話等，都有增加的趨勢。因此秘書這個職業也極被看好。

然而，只要有英文能力就能勝任女秘書的工作嗎？當然不是的。舉個例子來說吧，有位某公司的主管因公務出國，在外國看到許多有能力的女秘書，回國之後便指示徵求外語女秘書，但是他雇用的女秘書除了是個英文人才外，對於秘書的工作，處理的事務範圍絲毫不明瞭，最後不得不自行提出辭呈。

秘書的職務

秘書究竟必須做些什麼？確切來說，秘書的工作範圍委實不可小覷，其負責的職責也攸關重大，下表即從 5 個 W 1 個 H 的角度分別說明之。

WHO	是重要人物（上司）的秘書
WHEN	有強烈的時間觀念
WHERE	居於資訊網的中樞位置
WHAT	輔佐上司
WHY	使上司的業務順利
HOW	1. 管理上司的辦公室
	2. 安排上司的活動表
	3. 接待客戶
	4. 電話應對
	5. 會議的準備
	6. 安排上司出差的諸種事務
	7. 資料的蒐集與管理
	8. 文件處理
	9. 收發信件
	10. 其　他

秘書是資料處理專家

更詳細地說，WHAT 也就是秘書的機能，在輔佐的地位上，可以按上司的指示，代行上司的職務，但是沒有決定權，就秘書存在的理由，卽WHY 來說，為了讓上司能在主管職務上專心處理業務，秘書對蒐集的資料，必須加以取捨選擇，為上司在業務上先整理出脈絡。其具體內容就是HOW所提示的各項細目。

WHEN除了仔細編定已決定的工作（ *routine work* ）之外，就突然發生的 non-routine work 該何時處理，也要能決定其 priority （優先順序）。此外，站在上司的立場，瞭解各項事務的梗概，率先準備妥當以能適時處理的先見之明，也是在WHEN這一點上，對秘書的要求之一。

就WHERE 來說，秘書居於各種資料傳達的地位，相當於上司四周資訊網的中樞位置。至於WHO── 是重要人物（上司）的秘書這一點來說，「上司」在台灣可能僅限於 top management （最高經營者──主管級以上），但是在歐美則普及至 middle management （中級管理階層，經理級），甚至 lower management （部門管理階層，主任、科長級）。

提到WHO就想到為上司工作（ *work for the boss* ），但是，現在外國的秘書學校，除了教授 work for the boss，更進而指導 **work with the boss** 。是的，秘書必須共識的新觀念是，除了服務上司外，更須成為一個良好的工作伙伴。

以上逐一分析說明之後，再把秘書形象化並加以闡釋的話，則為：「秘書就是在身員重任的上司（WHO）之旁，周遭資訊網的中樞要津（WHERE），有時間觀念（WHEN）地加以輔佐（WHAT），使上司工作順利（WHY）的資料處理（HOW）專家。」

因此，秘書若沒有資料處理專家，那種對各種溝通方式的概念，就不會成為真正的專門秘書。

秘書必備的秉性與能力

　　對於秘書在資賦上的要求，如明晰的頭腦、**敏於應變**、**冷靜**、**謙虛**、有氣度、辦事能力強、效率高等等，眞是不勝枚舉。

　　然而，經過統計資料顯示，在職的秘書們認爲，最重要的一項秉賦就是 **initiative**（進取心），她們認爲幫助工作忙碌的上司，不是等指示下了才去做，而是自己率先處理安排，積極地加以輔助。因此，具備有 intitiative，卽可象徵此秘書能力過人；**在衆多條件中**，最能博取上司信賴，最能表現傑出者，也是 initiative。

　　以下列出的是，一般公認的優秀秘書應具有的秉性，供讀者參考並截人之長，補己之短。

【秘書秉性】

1. 明朗的性格
2. 積極的態度
3. 有協調的能力
4. 適當的禮儀
5. 謙虛
6. 正確的措辭
7. 合宜的服裝儀容
8. 優雅的儀態
9. 有強烈的時間觀念
10. 可調適自己的情緒
11. 有責任感
12. 有實踐力

13. 傑出的表達能力
14. 有理解、判斷的能力
15. 精神集中
16. 有遠見
17. 有企劃能力
18. 做事確實
19. 記性好
20. 有高度保密能力
21. 身體健康

第2章

秘書英語必備常識

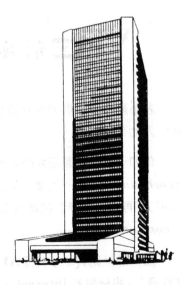

商業書信的重點

秘書必須經常要把上司口述的東西筆記下來，或將上司錄好的東西打成信件。因此，秘書必須具備藉由打字、速記或其他方法做筆記的技術，更應該有爲上司撰寫文案的能力。

譬如當秘書知道，上司收到謝函或書信而遲遲未作覆，那麼就應該機警地自擬文案，如 "I have drafted a thank-you note to Mr. Bright. Will you be able to use it?"（我已擬妥一封給布萊特先生的謝函，可以派上用場嗎？），呈示上司，或許因此而使您有機會擔任更加重要的事務。

以下就來談談英文商業書信的書寫重點，俾能讓您學到更完美溝通的技巧。

信函的架構

若不經修飾，劈頭就寫這封信的目的，是非常不智的，應該預先考慮信函的架構。

例如，當你寫說服式的書信，可以考慮使用 *general-specific-conclusion*（一般－明確－結論）的方式。即先表示一般性的看法（*general*），再指出這種看法吻合現在所談的事（*specific*），最後導向結論（*conclusion*）。

如果是推銷貨品，就採 **AIDA** 的方式，首先引起讀者的 attention（注意），再使他有 interest（興趣），而後引起對方的購買 desire

（慾望），最後導向購買的 action（行動）。或者也可以考慮用 **4 Ps**，即 Picture（描寫），Promise（允諾），Prove（證明），and Push（驅使）的結構。

　　所有信函中以**拒絕函**為最難。第一段要感謝對方的來信，做成 buffer zone（緩衝地帶），將肯定的部分敘述於前，然後在第二段中表明本意，最後寫上若有機會請再惠予指教。也就是用肯定的段落夾著否定的內容。任何信件的結尾語都必須爽快而坦誠。

★★★ 牢記 6Cs 的原則 ★★★

　　6Cs 即 correctness（正確），completeness（完整），clearness（清晰），conciseness（簡潔），consideration（體貼），courtesy（有禮）的六個 C 。

(1) correct（正確）且 complete（完整）的信函

　　商業文書絕不容許有誤。若數字或其他內容有誤就失去其身為資料的價值，而且因疏忽造成的錯誤也會使對方失去信心。若文章無誤卻丟三忘四，或者沒有遺漏但卻重點不明，令人不知所云，這樣的信函其價值也已減去大半。要做到 Completeness，可以 **5 個 W 1 個 H**：Who（何人），When（何時），Where（何地），What（何事），Why（原因），How（方式）為書寫目標，留心結構要領，並務使結論明確。

(2) clear（清晰）concise（簡潔）的信函

　　以往的商用書信喜歡用生硬的寫法及客套話。其實，在商業上，平易洗鍊的用法、簡明扼要的文句才是必備條件。例如，把 *at the time of this writing* 改寫成 now，把 *owing to the fact that* 改成 because，是不是簡潔多了？！clear、concise 的信函，不但減少書寫者的麻煩，更節省了閱信人的時間。

若說前面提及的 correctness（正確）和 completeness（完整）是掌握了商業書信的基本價值，那麼 clearness（清晰）和 conciseness（簡潔）則與商業書信的經濟性習習相關。

(3) considerate（體貼），courteous（有禮）的筆觸

以上兩段中所談及的四個 C，在商場上，幾乎是不可或缺的要件，有時只須用這 4 個 C 就能完成一封優秀的商業書信。但是，如果要潤飾人際之間的磨擦，就得靠 consideration（體貼）了。例如 Thank you very much for your letter of....（謝謝您…來信）就比 We received your letter of.....（我方收到您…來信），比較容易引起共鳴。

此外，這種稱為*You attitude*（第二人稱的心態）的技巧，是站在對方的立場下陳述我方的意願，對於提高溝通效果來說，非常重要。

courtesy（有禮）和 consideration（體貼），在意見上沒什麼差別，然而卻更予人鄭重之感。有志於以秘書為職業者，在正確、完整、清晰、簡潔之外，更需學會商業書信彬彬有禮且格調高雅的用法，才能發揮潛能，出類拔萃，獲得上司的賞識。

★★★ 商業書信的視覺技巧 ★★★

文書不比口頭交涉，無法視對方的反應加以說明，又不能展示直接、具體的東西。為了彌補這項缺點，利用照片、樣品、圖表等，使對方易於

了解是非常必要的。

此外，諸如迅卽訴諸視覺的**主題寫法**、**條列式**、**劃線**等，都是使對方易於把握內容的技巧。還有，**信函版面的優美**，**打字的功夫**，都足以表現出秘書的能力如何。

儘量避免否定用法

在前面我們已提過，把 negative 用法夾藏於 positive 用法之中，至少語氣上婉轉得多，也算表示對於對方立場的 consideration（體貼）。例如

Thank you for calling our attention to the late arrival of....
　謝謝您提醒我方注意…的延誤

就比

We have received your complaint about the late arrival of....
　我方已收到貴方對於…延誤的抱怨

來得落落大方，穩當而妥貼。信函之中要極力避免使用 no（不），cannot（不能），claim（索賠），complaint（抱怨），inefficiency（無效率），等否定字眼。

注意書信版面

書信的版面及格式，決定於個人喜好或各公司的規定，但是不要忽視了配合時代感。

✠ 商業書信格式

在重視效率的現代，一般都用 *modified-block style*（改良式，住址、謙稱及簽名等齊頭，信文則採鋸齒式）或 *full-block style*（各段左側皆對齊，不右縮）（參考以下範例）。日期各行及本文各段落，需向內縮入數格的 indented style（鋸齒式），耗時費事，已漸不採用。

此外，可依信文長短，調整上下、左右的空間，務使版面好比一幅圖畫般，穩重的放在畫框中央一般。

✠ 標點符號

至於標點符號，現在普遍使用 salutation（抬頭）和 complimentary close（結尾祝辭）後面，不加冒號和逗點的 open punctuation（不加標點），這樣比較一般化，同時也是顧慮效率的緣故。

✠ 日期的寫法

日期的寫法上，美式把月份放在前面

　　May 7, 19—

英式則把日期放在前面

　　7th May, 19—

爲求效率，英式也用

　　7 May, 19—，用這種寫法的公司越來越多。

✠ 商業書信有愈形簡化的趨勢

從效益觀點來看，照理說 full-block style（齊頭式），open punctuation（不加標點）最合乎經濟原則。但近來有一種更爲簡單的 *simplified style*（簡化式），就是不寫 salutation（抬頭）在 inside address（對方地址姓名）之後空一行直接書寫 body（本文）。信末也不寫 complimentary close（結尾祝辭）直接簽名。但是，在曉得收信人姓名時，通常要在本文第一行稱呼對方，以示禮貌。

這種 simplified style（簡化式）的信函，適用於認爲將稱呼寫成 Gentlemen 太忽視女性，寫成 Ladies and Gentlemen 則像是演講人士使用的情況。

不過，簡化式的信函仍然符合，左端對齊書寫的 full-block style（齊頭式）。

長達兩頁的信函（ 2-page letter ）的接續法，以下即有範例供讀者參考。

```
MR JAMES HWANG
3-2 TUN HWA SOUTH ROAD
TAIPEI TAIWAN
ROC
                        MR ROBERT J JACKSON
                        3333 E HASKELL AVENUE
                        DALLAS TX 75204
                        USA
```

▨ Modified-block Style 改良式

PACIFIC FOODSTUFFS COMPANY

3-2, Tun Hwa South Road, Taipei, Taiwan,
R.O.C.
Phone：(02)7116854 Telex：5422116 Cable：
FOODOS

May 7 ,19—

Mr. James R. Kelston, Manager
Overseas Operations
Food Services, Incorporated
100 Wacker Drive
Chicago, Illinois 60606
U.S.A.

Dear Mr. Kelston

Thank you very much for your letter of
April 15. Your proposal that our companies form a joint venture to establish a
chain of waffle and pancake restaurants
in Taiwan is a very welcome one and we
believe it has great potential.

I will be in Chicago for two weeks from
June 15 and would very much like to meet
with you to discuss this matter in more
detail. I will ask our Los Angeles office
to arrange an appointment and am looking
forward to seeing you next month.

Sincerely

James Hwang

James Hwang
Vice-President

JH:HS
cc: Mr. Thomas Chao, Los Angeles Branch Office

▨ Full-block Style 齊頭式

PACIFIC FOODSTUFFS COMPANY

3-2, Tun Hwa South Road, Taipei, Taiwan,
R.O.C.
Phone : 7116854 Telex : 5422116 Cable :
FOODOS

May 7, 19——

Mr. James R. Kelston, Manager
Overeas Operations
Food Services, Incorporated
100 Wacker Drive
Chicago, Illinois 60606
U.S.A.

Dear Mr. Kelston

Thank you very much for your letter of
April 15. Your proposal that our companies form a joint venture to establish a
chain of waffle and pancake restaurants
in Taiwan is a very welcome one and we
believe it has great potential.

I will be in Chicago for two weeks from
June 15 and would very much like to meet
with you to discuss this matter in more
detail. I will ask our Los Angeles office
to arrange an appointment and am looking
forward to seeing you next month.

Sincerely yours

James Hwang

James Hwang
Vice-President

jh/hs
cc: Mr. Thomas Chao, Los Angeles Branch Office

▨ Semi-block Style 折衷式

PACIFIC FOODSTUFFS COMPANY

3-2, Tun Hwa South Road, Taipei, Taiwan,
R.O.C.
Phone : 7116854 Telex : 5422116 Cable :
FOODOS

Mr. James R. Kelston, Manager
Overseas Operations
Food Services, Incorporated
100 Wacker Drive
Chiago   Illinois 60606
U.S.A
Dear Mr. Kelston:

    Thank you very much for your letter
of April 15. Your proposal that our
companies form a joint venture to establish a chain of waffle and pancake restaurants in Taiwan is a very welcome one
and we believe it has great potential.

    I will be in Chicago for two weeks
from June 15 and would very much like to
meet with you to discuss this matter in
more detail. I will ask our Los Angeles
office to arrange an appointment and am
looking forward to seeing you next month.

                Very truly yours,

                James Hwang

                James Hwang
                Vice-President

JH/HS
cc: Mr. Thomas Chao, Los Angeles Branch Office

■ 2-Page Letter 長達兩頁的信函

PACIFIC FOODSTUFFS COMPANY

3-2, Tun Hwa South Road, Taipei, Taiwan,
R.O.C.
Phone : 7116854 Telex : 5422116 Cable :
FOODOS

May 7, 19——

Mr. James R. Kelston, Manager
Overseas Operations
Food Services, Incorporated
100 Wacker Drive
Chicago, Illinois 60606
U.S.A.

Dear Mr. Kelston:

Thank you very much for your letter of
April 15. Your proposal that our companies form a joint venture to establish a
chain of waffle and pancake restaurants
in Taiwan is a very welcome one and we
believe it has great potential.

As you are well aware, a number of
American fast food chains are already
doing business in Taiwan. Their success seems to be based largely on good
management and skillful merchandising.

We believe that to be successful a waffle and pancake restaurant chain should
follow the same pattern, and retain as
many American-style operating procedures
as possible. Although the initial capital
investment will be great, economies of
scale will bear fruit in the long run.

Mr. James R. Kelston

Page 2

May 7, 19 ——

Further, it is the opinion of our staff that every effort be made to retain the taste and flavor variety of the American product, as this is most likely to appeal to young people who will make up the bulk of the customers.

I will be in the United States for about two weeks from June 15 and would very much like to meet with you to discuss this matter in more detail.

My tentative schedule is as follows:

Los Angeles	June 15-20
Denver	June 21-22
Chicago	June 23-26
New York	June 27-30
Los Angeles	July 1-2

I will ask our Los Angeles office to arrange an appointment and am looking forward to seeing you next month.

Sincerely,

James Hwang

James Hwang
Vice-President

JH:HS
cc: Mr. Thomas Chao, Los Angeles Branch Office

書寫信封的新規則

　　書寫版面極其均衡的信封，除了給人良好印象之外，更重要的原因乃是配合郵政業務電腦處理信件，考慮電腦的 Read Zone（閱讀地帶）的需要所致。Read Zone 在信封的 Lower Right Quarter（右下的四分之一），所以要從信封的中央，開始向右橫寫，跟信封上下兩端平行，右側和下端至少要保留 $\frac{1}{2}$ 英吋（約 1.25 公分）的空白。

　　爲了便於電腦閱讀，收件人姓名地址的寫法必須統一。第一行寫姓名，第二行寫地區，Street（街），Avenue（大道；大街），Drive（車道），P.O.Box（郵政信箱）等，第三行寫市名、州名（可用簡寫），郵遞區號，最後一行寫國名，如下所示（要特別注意全部大寫，並省略所有標點符號）。

MR　ROBERT　J　JACKSON

3333 E　HASKELL　AVENUE

DALLAS　TX　75204

USA

　　這項規則可能隨著科技進展，時有更動，所以要不時注意最新的 The World Almanac（世界年鑑）。

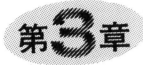

第3章

秘書求職與面談

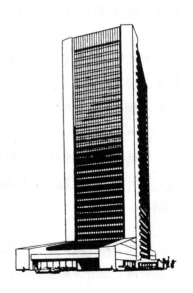

怎樣找到求職的門路？

專心攻**讀**英文，想在說英文的單位謀個職位者大有人在，但要怎樣才能找到求職的門路呢？卻有許多人不知從何著手。

開發求職門路有兩種方法：
 ㈠ **透過職業輔導中心介紹。**
 ㈡ **利用中、英文報紙的廣告。**

在各職業輔導中心，通常是要先瞭解一下您的英語程度和打字能力，而後登記，再以各公司所需要的對象，分別介紹前往任職。其次可看中、英文報紙的求人廣告欄（*Help Wanted Ad*），再以電話、寫信或親往應徵。甚至可以自己在報上登出求職廣告（*Situation Wanted*）。

對於雙語秘書（*bilingual secretary*）的需求，還是以台北的公司居多，至於中南部所需，相形之下就減少了許多。不過，雙語秘書愈形重要，則是不爭的事實，也是必然的趨勢。

面試時一定要帶著（或是郵寄）履歷表。其實，歐美各國對於入公司之前的筆試並不太重視，大多視**履歷表、推薦信**和**面談**三者作最後決定的標準。

因此，寫一張漂漂亮亮的履歷表及應徵信函，同時對面談時的技巧多加領會，都是非常重要的。本章即針對此，專就面談技巧這一方面，

EMPLOYMENT

Taiwanese female (20)
seeks position in Taipei
area as bilingual secretary.
Fluent English; U.S. High
School experience. Typing
and secretarial training.
Tel: 3930152

HELP WANTED

A Taiwan Trade Co.
urgently requires female,
age 30-40, good command
of English and excellent
typing skills. Experience
as secretary highly pref-
erable. Salary and other
terms in accordance with
company regulations. 5-
day week. Please mail
P.O. Box 5532, Taipei,
Taiwan, R.O.C.

FOREIGN BANK requires
female secretary cum
stenographer with good
command of spoken and
written English. Short-
hand speed 100 wpm and
typing speed 60 wpm.
Previous experience min-
imum 5 years. Apply
with full particulars in-
cluding photograph and
details of past expe-
rience, etc. to 3-2 Tun
Hwa South Road, Tai-
pei.

做詳盡的說明，至於求職、應徵信函，本書「模範秘書英語書信」一章有
詳細的示範及練習。

★★★ 秘書面談的技巧 ★★★

面談時要注意的各點，說明如下：

❈ 面談之前

1. 先調查一下欲前往面試的公司或團體，其企業涵蓋的範圍、性質、
   規模、特徵等。

2. 應事先整理一下，確定如何表達自己的資格、能力及特點（所
   說的絕不可與履歷表上寫的東西相左）。

3. 預先準備對方可能問什麼問題，並準備好答案。

4. 準備好合宜的面試服裝，在前往面談之前，必須有充分的時間，
   好好整理一下自己的儀容。

5. 先調查一下一般秘書的薪水。

　　就薪資一項來說，東、西方人所持的態度不盡相同。歐美人有自
行表示意願的習慣，就職時一定清楚地說明希望待遇。東方人則總是
畏畏縮縮，不知所措。但是，須牢記千萬不要說「給多少都沒關係」，
以免雙方徒增困擾。

✂ 面談時

1. 　　第一眼的招呼、問候語相當重要，可頷首並說 "Good Morning, Sir. My name is Wendy Wu. How do you do?"不必握手。若聽到親切的問候 "Very nice to see you."等等，應該視情況回答 "Thank you for giving me this opportunity."之類的話。

　　爲了附和對方所說，不時在句子中加上 "Ya, ya."等附和用語，這種俗氣、應聲蟲式的說法，現在已不多用了。

2. 　　若對方說 "Please have a seat."，可大方地說句 "Thank you."而後坐下。注意坐姿，背脊需稍挺，不要整個靠在椅背上，其他無意識的舉動，如玩弄頭髮、抖腿等千萬得防範出現，務必給人沉著、穩健的印象。

3. 　　談話中間不要東張西望，而應在重點處,注視對方眼神侃侃而談。

4. 　　對於對方的詢問，不能單是回答 "Yes."或者 "No."，應該就主題多談談自己的意見，尤其主持面試者是歐、美人士時，更是需要如此。

　　此外，切忌完全否定的回答，更積極的答覆問題才是正確的態度。

　　例如，當你被問及："Can you operate a word processor?"（你會操作文字處理機嗎？）而你完全沒有經驗，此時，絕不可以只答 "No."，而應該說：

"No, but I am very much interested in learning how to
operate a word processor. I have been trained in operating an
accounting machine and telex, and I'm sure I can learn it
quickly."

「沒有，但是我對學習如何操作文字處理機，非常有興趣。我在收
銀機及電傳打字方面曾經受過訓練，而且我確信將能很快地學會。」

5. 面試結束時的標準形式 —— 最後主試者一定會說 "We'll let
you know what we decide in a few days. Thank you very
much for coming."

「幾天內會通知你我們的決定,非常謝謝你能來面試。」"

你則應客氣地說聲 "Thank you, Mr～." 而後走出來。

以下是主考官對應徵者面試的評價表 (*Interview Rating Form*)，
包含有各項目的評審，可供讀者參考。

INTERVIEW RATING FORM 面談計分表			
A. INTERVIEW SKILLS	good	fair	poor
1. Clothes and grooming	√		
2. Posture, body control and eye contact	√		
3. Language	√		

	good	fair	poor
4. Manners and breeding	√		
5. Preparation		√	
B. PERSONALITY	good	fair	poor
1. Motivation	√		
2. Attitude towards self		√	
3. Potential	√		
C. QUALIFICATIONS	good	fair	poor
1. Skills and training		√	
2. Experience and background			√

✦ 各項目的注意要點如下。首先談 Interview Skill 。

1. Clothes and grooming: neat, clean, suitable for the interview
   衣著打扮：整齊、乾淨、適合面談的場合

2. Posture, body control and eye contact
   儀態、身體的控制和眼睛的接觸

3. Language: polite and appropriate; careful listening and appropriate responses to questions
   語言：有禮且合宜；仔細傾聽並合宜地回答問題

4. Manners and breeding: politeness and adult behavior
   禮貌和教養：有禮及成熟的舉止

5. Preparation: how well the applicant is informed about the company and the job requirements
準備：應徵者對公司和工作的要求知道的多寡

✦ Personality 性格

1. Motivation: the degree to which the applicant really desires the job
動機：應徵者真正希望得到這份工作的程度

2. Attitude towards self : the applicant should be modest but be willing to mention his / her strong points and admit weak points 對自我的態度：應徵者應該謙虛，但願意提到他（她）的優點並承認其弱點。

3. Potential: the degree to which the applicant is likely to succeed in the job if hired
潛力：應徵者如果被錄取工作可能勝任的程度

✦ Qualifications 資格

Skills , training, experience and background that will help the applicant perform the job well
會幫助應徵者把工作做好的技能、訓練、經驗和背景

秘書面談實例

　　以下是太平洋食品公司應徵秘書中的複選者李莉莉，人事主任的助理哈利·威爾森先生與她面談。威爾森先生的面談重點是評斷英語會話實力。

以下是面談典型問答，並有不懂詢問內容，請求覆述一次的情況。

JOB INTERVIEW

W： Come in. My name is Harry Wilson. How do you do?
請進。我的名字叫哈利・威爾森。妳好嗎？

L： My name is Lily Lee. How do you do?
我的名字叫李莉莉。您好嗎？

W： Please have a seat. 請坐。

L： Thank you. 謝謝您。

W： Let me ask you a few questions, Miss Lee. Where do you live? 李小姐，請教妳一些問題。妳住在哪裏？

L： I live in Taipei. 我住在台北。

W： Taipei, I see. And where are you going to school?
台北，我了解了。妳在哪裡上學？

L： I go to Soochow University. 我上東吳大學。

W： Where is that? 在哪裡呢？

L： I beg your pardon? 對不起，請再說一次。

W： Where is Soochow University? In what city?
東吳大學在哪裡？在什麼城市？

L： Oh, it's in Taipei. 噢，在台北。

W： And what is your major? 妳主修什麼？

L： I'm majoring in English. 我主修英文。

W : I see. Have you taken any business classes or anything?
我了解了。妳曾經修過商業課程或其它科目嗎?

L : Yes, I've taken typing and Secretarial Theory and this
year I'm taking Secretarial Practice and Current
English. 是的,我曾經修過打字和秘書理論,今年我修秘書實
務和現代英文。

W : Have you ever worked in an office before?
妳曾經上過班嗎?

L : Yes, I had a part-time job for two months at International Trading Co.
我曾在國際貿易公司工讀兩個月。

W : Oh, really? 噢,真的嗎?

L : Yes, it was a very interesting experience.
是的,那是很有趣的經驗。

W : What did you do, office work?
妳做什麼,辦公室工作嗎?

L : Yes, mostly typing and running errands.
是的,主要是打字和外務。

W : Oh, very good, very good. But you know that we are
really looking for a bilingual secretary. Why did you
answer our ad?
噢,很好,很好。但是妳知道我們實際上要找的是能說兩種語
言的秘書,妳爲什麼應徵我們的廣告呢?

L：Well, for me the most important thing is to find work where I can meet with and deal with people from other cultures. As a Chinese, this seems to be the most exciting thing I can do. 唔，對我來說，最重要的是找一份可以碰到來自其他文化的人，和他們打交道的工作。身爲中國人，這似乎是我所能做的最令人興奮的事。

W：I see. Of course, you've been overseas, haven't you? 我了解了。當然，妳曾經出過國，不是嗎？

L：Yes, I've been to America. I lived in Wisconsin on a home-stay program. 是的，在一項住在外國家庭計劃的安排之下，我曾去過美國，住在威斯康辛州。

W：Oh, really？ How long were you there？ 噢，眞的嗎？妳在那兒待了多久？

L：Eleven months, when I was in high school. 十一個月，當時我在讀高中。

W：Oh, wonderful. No wonder you speak English so well. And you must be used to dealing with foreigners. 噢，眞棒。難怪妳英文講得這麼好，妳一定很習慣和外國人交往。

L：Yes, I am, to some extent. 是的，某種程度的交往。

W：Good. Now, do you have any questions you'd like to ask me about this company？ 很好。現在，關於這家公司，妳有沒有任何問題想問我？

L：Yes, I would like to ask about the salary. How is it determined？ 有的，我想問有關薪資的問題。它是如何決定的？

W: Well, all new clerical employees begin at a standard salary of 12,000 dollars per month. Then, after your training period, you are given an assignment. Someone like yourself may be given a higher-ranking assignment, and then you would get a higher monthly salary.

唔，所有新雇用的辦事員以每月一萬二千元的標準薪開始。然後，在訓練期之後，妳會被指派工作。有些像妳這樣的人可能派給職位較高的工作，而且妳會得到更高的月薪。

L: What about other benefits? 其他的福利怎麼樣呢？

W: All employees must join the health insurance program, and there are many other benefits. I think that most of them are explained in our brochure. Did you get a copy?

所有的職員必須加入健康保險計劃，還有其他許多福利。我想大部分福利我們的小冊子上都有說明。妳有一本嗎？

L: Yes, I did. Thank you. 是的，我有。謝謝您。

W: Any more questions? 還有問題嗎？

L: No, I'm sorry to have taken up so much of your time.

沒有，我很抱歉佔用您這麼多時間。

W: Not at all. Very glad to have met you. We'll be letting you know the result of the interview sometime next week. Thank you very much for coming.

不客氣。很高興見到妳。下星期某個時候我們會讓妳知道面談的結果。非常謝謝妳來。

C : Thank you very much for giving me your time, Mr. Wilson.

非常感謝您給我時間，威爾森先生。

W : You're quite welcome. Good-by. 別客氣。再見。

C : Good-by. 再見。

X Sample Interview Questions and Model Answers :

1. What is your full name, please? 請告訴我妳的全名。

   Lily Wu. 吳莉莉。

2. Where do you live? 妳住在哪裏？

   I live in Yungho, a suburb of Taipei.

   我住永和，在台北近郊。

3. Where were you born? 妳在哪裏出生？

   I was born in Yen Cheng, in Kaohsiung.

   我出生於高雄塩埕。

4. What is your major at school? 妳在學校主修什麼？

   I'm majoring in English. 我主修英文。

5. What kind of courses are you taking?

   妳正在修那些課程呢？

   I have many English courses, such as reading, oral
   English, composition and so on. Also, I take some
   general education courses like history, law and art.

   我有許多英文課，像閱讀、口語的英文、作文等等。我
   也選修一些普通的教育課程，像歷史、法律和藝術。

6. Do you get any special training in secretarial skills?
   妳有沒有受過任何有關秘書技能的特殊訓練？

   > Yes, last year I took Secretarial Theory and this
   > year I'm taking Secretarial Practice. I've also had
   > typing, Current English, Business English and
   > similar courses.
   > 有的，我去年修秘書理論，今年正在修秘書實務。我也
   > 修過打字、現代英文、商業英文和類似的課程。

7. Can you operate a Chinese typewriter?
   你會操作中文打字機嗎？

   > No, I am sorry, but I have studied English typing.
   > 抱歉，我不會，但是我修過英文打字。

---

8. What about work experience? Have you had any part-time
   jobs?
   工作經驗如何呢？你曾經工讀過嗎？

   > Just one, one summer when I did office work.
   > 只有一次，有個夏天我做辦公室工作。

9. Have you ever done any selling, or teaching as a tutor?
   你曾經賣過東西或當家教嗎？

   > No, I haven't, except for helping my brother with
   > English. When I was in America, I taught some
   > girls flower arrangement at school.
   > 不，我不曾，除了幫助我弟弟讀英文。我在美國時，曾
   > 經在學校教一些女孩子插花。

10. What are your hobbies? What do you like to do in your spare time? 妳的嗜好是什麼？妳閒暇時喜歡做什麼？

    Well, I like reading, and listening to music — especially American folk songs. I play the guitar a little, and I like the movies, too.

    唔，我喜歡讀書和聽音樂—尤其是美國民謠。彈吉他我會一點，也喜歡看電影。

11. What do you like best about school?

    課業方面，你最喜歡什麼？

    The oral English classes. We get a lot of chances to speak English.

    英文會話課。我們有許多機會說英文。。

---

12. Why did you choose this company?

    你爲什麼選擇這家公司呢？

    Well, I know that you do a very big international business, so I thought it would be a good place for me to use the experience I've had living overseas.

    嗯，我知道貴公司在國貿方面的生意做得很大，所以我想這裏會是運用我在國外獲得的經驗的好地方。

13. Do you want to work here because you can speak English?

    你是因爲可以說英文而想在這裏工作嗎？

No', not just because I can speak English. What I really want is the chance to know myself better as a Chinese by dealing with and trying to understand foreigners. 不，不只是因爲可以說英文。我眞正希望的是想藉著和外國人打交道，和試著了解他們，更加瞭解身爲中國人的自己。

14. What are your plans for the future?

妳對未來的計畫是什麼？

I'd like to continue working as long as I can. It's becoming more and more common among young couples for both the husband and wife to work, and I think that Chinese men will be helping more with the household chores, the way they do in America.

我想只要我可以就繼續工作。年輕夫婦中丈夫和妻子都在工作變得越來越普遍，我認爲中國男人會愈來愈幫著做家庭雜務，像在美國一樣。

15. Do you think you will want to continue working here even after you've had children?

妳想甚至在妳有小孩之後，會繼續在這裏工作嗎？

Well, that's a long time in the future. I don't know what my thinking will be then.

唔，那是很久以後的事。我不知道那時候我的想法如何。

X Questions that the applicant might ask the interviewer :

· What type of work will I be expected to do at first?

　剛開始我會被派任哪一種工作呢？

· Do you have a training program for new employees?

　貴公司對新進職員有訓練課程嗎？

· Are most of your foreign customers Americans or do they come from many different countries?

　貴公司大部分的外國客戶是美國人呢，還是來自許多不同國家？

· Can you tell me a little bit about employee benefits such as the health insurance program?

　您能告訴我一點關於健康保險計劃之類的員工福利嗎？

· What are the normal working hours?

　正常上班時間是幾小時？

· Will I be expected to work late very often?

　我得經常工作到很晚嗎？

· Do you have recreational activities or study groups for employees?

　貴公司有員工娛樂活動或讀書小組嗎？

X What to say when you do not understand the interviewer :

· I beg your pardon? 對不起，請再說一次。

· I'm sorry, but I don't understand your meaning.

> 對不起，我不了解您的意思。

· Would you mind saying（asking）that again, please?

> 請再說（問）一次好嗎？

· Would you mind saying（asking）that again a bit more slowly, please?

> 請您速度慢一些覆述（再問）一次好嗎？

· I'm not sure I understood your question.

> 我不確定是否了解您的問題。

第4章

模範秘書英語書信

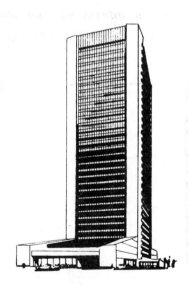

1) 求職與應聘

1. 應徵求才廣告

【秘書須知】

- *apply for* ☞　申請；應徵

- *among my courses* ☞　在我修過的課程中

- *major in* ☞　專攻；主修

- *for additional information regarding ～*
  ☞　另外，關於～的參考資料

- *refer to* ☞　查詢

- *grant me an interview* ☞　答應接見我；給我面談的機會

- *an addressed and stamped envelope*
  ☞　寫明地址的回郵信封

實　例

Shu-fen Chiang

No, 33, 4F, Lane 112,

Tung Hwa Street,

Taipei, Taiwan,

R.O.C.

October 5, 19 —

Personnel Manager

Pfizer Ltd.

No. 215, 10 F, Tun Hwa North Road

Taipei, Taiwan

R.O.C.

Dear Sir,

In reply to your advertisement in today's China Times I am applying for the position of shorthand-typist. I am twenty-two years of age and will graduate from Fu-Jen Catholic University in June, 19 —.

I have been studying English for the past four years. Among my courses, I majored in Business English and Secretarial English and acquired a keen interest in these subjects.

I would very much like the opportunity to work in your company and convert my knowledge and keen interest to practical use.

I am enclosing a full personal history. For additional information regarding my personal qualifcations, please refer to Mr. Ming Lee, Professor of English at Departmant of English, Fu-Jen Catholic University, located at 510 Chung Cheng Road, Hsin

Chuang, Taipei Hsien, R.O.C. I should be grateful
if you would grant me an interview.

I enclose an addressed and stamped envelope for
your reply.

Respectfully yours

Shu-fen chiang

🖂　答覆貴公司今天在中國時報刊登的廣告，我寫這封信應徵速記員的職
位。我今年22歲，19—年六月將從輔仁大學畢業。

過去四年來，我一直研讀英文，在我修過的課程中，我專攻商業
英文和秘書英語，並且從這些科目獲得強烈的興趣。

我非常希望能在貴公司服務，把所學和強烈的興趣，轉變成實際
應用。

茲附上個人全部的經歷，另外，關於我個人適任與否的參考資料，
請向輔仁大學英語系英文教授李民先生查詢，地址是台北縣新莊市，
中正路510號，輔仁大學。我將感激貴公司給我面談的機會。

為了方便您回覆起見，隨信附上寫明地址的回郵信封一個。

【註】　acquire〔əˈkwaɪr〕*v*. 得；獲得
　　　　keen〔kin〕*adj*. 強烈的；熱心的
　　　　secretarial〔͵sɛkrəˈtɛrɪəl〕*adj*. 秘書的
　　　　convert〔kənˈvɝt〕*v*. 轉變；改變

2. 履歷表範例

【 秘書須知 】

- *I (hereby) certify that the above statement is true and correct to the best of my knowledge and belief.*

  ☞　我（藉此）保證上列敍述眞實無誤，皆就我所知，盡我所信而言。

實例 (1)

PERSONAL HISTORY

PERSONAL INFORMATION

Name:	Shu-fen Chiang
Present Address:	No.33, 4F, Lane 112, Tung Hwa Street, Taipei, Taiwan, R.O.C.
Home Address:	No.61, Lane 251, Chung Cheng Road, Keelung, Taiwan, R.O.C.
Date of Birth:	September 10, 19—(age：22)
Family Relation:	First daughter of Chan-chien Chiang
Height:	160 cm.
Weight:	50 kg.

Marital Status:	Single

EDUCATIONAL RECORD

19—~19—	Chung-Cheng Junior High School
19—~19—	Chung-Shan Girls' Senior High School
19—	Admitted to Department of English of Fu-Jen Catholic University
June, 19—	Will graduate from the above University

WORK EXPERIENCE   None

SPECIAL SKILLS & TECHNICAL QUALIFICATION

Awarded first prize in the all R.O.C. Intercollegiate English Oratorial Contest for 19—.

A thorough academic training in Business English and Secretarial English

A conscientious training in typing, 60 w.p.m.

Reference: Prof. Ming Lee, Department of English, Fu-Jen Catholic University.

I hereby certify that the above statement is true and correct to the best of my knowledge and belief.

October 5, 19—

Shu-fen Chiang

個人經歷

個人資料

姓名：	江淑芬
現在地址：	台北市通化街112巷33號4F
永久地址：	基隆市中正路251巷61號
出生日期：	19—,9月10日（22歲）
家屬關係：	江俊傑的長女
身高：	160公分
體重：	50公斤
婚姻狀況：	單身

教育紀錄

19—～19— 就讀於中正國中

19—～19— 就讀於中山女中

19— 進入輔仁大學英語系

19— 6月 將畢業於上述大學

工作經驗 無

特殊才能及技藝資格

19—全國大專院校英語演講比賽獲得第一名。

受過商業英文和秘書英語徹底的學院式訓練

受過打字的完全訓練，一分鐘60個字

保證人： 輔仁大學英語系李民教授

藉此我保證上列敍述眞實無誤，皆就我所知，盡我所信而言。

江淑芬　19—，11 月 5 日

✦　　　✦　　　✦

【註】　intercollegiate〔,ɪntəkə'lidʒɪɪt〕*adj.* 大學之間的
　　　　oratorial〔,ɔrə'tɔrɪəl〕*adj.* 演說的
　　　　award〔ə'wɔrd〕*v.* 授與

~~~~~~~~~~~~~~~~~~~~~~~~~~~~~~~~

【秘書須知】

- *Major Courses* ☞　主修科目
- *Minor Program* ☞　副修科目
- *Extracurricular Activities* ☞　課外活動
- *form letter* ☞　同文信函；複寫函件；印刷函件
- *laboratory data pertinent to sales*
　　☞　與銷售相關的試驗所資料
- *Made out payroll* ☞　謄寫薪水册
- *proofreading typeset copy* ☞　校對排字稿件
- *minor bookkeeping* ☞　次要簿記
- *screening phone calls* ☞　電話過濾
- *References available on request*
　　☞　身份保證人可供查詢

實例（2）

THE RESUME

Telephone
（02）3110452

Lily Wu
52 Peiping Road
Taipei, Taiwan, R.O.C.

EDUCATION

19—～19—	College of Commerce, Tamkang University. Bachelor of Science in Management.
Major Courses:	Management and Organizational Analysis, Behavioral Science, Computer-Based Management, Information System Analysis and Office Management.
Minor Program:	Courses in advertising, marketing, foreign trade and business communication.

EXTRACURRICULAR ACTIVITIES

Senior Class:	Vice-President
Speech Club:	Chairman
Student Newspaper:	Chief reporter

BUSINESS EXPERIENCE

19—～Present

Administrative Assistant and Executive Secretary to Vice President Mr. Henry Scott— Richmond Cosmetics, Inc.. Developed a series of form letters to respond to customer inquiries. Organized a system for recording laboratory data pertinent to sales. Present duties include handling a major part of the customer correspondence, and supervising four persons.

19—～19—

Secretary to the Overseas Manager—Mao Yuan Electric Company, Inc.. Handled telephone and written inquiries. Made out payroll. Typed correspondence.

19—～19—

Receptionist and typist—Ta Fang Advertising Agency. Was responsible for all general office work, which included filing, typing all correspondence, proofreading typeset copy, minor bookkeeping and screening phone calls.

```
ADDITIONAL              Traveled in Japan and U.S.A.
                        Fluent in Japanese. Inter-
                        ested in travel, swimming.

References:

        Professor Shing Wang
        Department of Commerce
        Tamkang University.
        Mr. Henry Scott
        Richmond Cosmetics, Inc.

References available on request.
```

履　歷　表

電話：（02）3110452

吳莉莉
台北市北平路52號
教育

19—～19—	淡江大學商學院管理科學學士。
主修科目	管理與組織分析，行爲科學，電腦基本管理，資訊系統分析，辦公室管理。
副修科目	廣告學，市場學，外貿，商業通訊等課程。

課外活動：

四年級：	副班代
演講社：	主席
學生報紙：	首要記者

商業經驗

19—～至今	利其蒙化粧品有限公司副董事長，亨利‧史考特先生的行政助理與執行秘書。
	曾發展一系列印刷函件，以答覆消費者的詢問。
	曾組織一系統，以記錄與銷售相關的試驗所資料。
	目前職務包括，處理大部份消費者信件，且管理四個人。
19——19—	懋源電器有限公司海外部經理秘書。
	處理電話和詢問函，謄寫薪水冊。打信件。
19——19—	大方廣告代理的接待員兼打字員。
	負責所有一般辦公室工作，包括檔案處理、所有信件的打字、校對排字稿件，次要簿記，及電話過濾。
其他：	曾旅遊日本、美國。日語流利。
	愛好旅遊與游泳。
身份保證人	淡江大學商學系王興教授
	利其蒙化粧品有限公司亨利‧史考特先生

身份保證人可供查詢

✦　　　✦　　　✦

【註】 behavioral 〔 bɪ'hevjərəl 〕 *adj*. 行為的

　　　receptionist 〔 rɪ'sɛpʃənɪst 〕 *n*. 接待員

　　　administrative 〔 əd'mɪnə,stretɪv 〕 *adj*. 行政的

　　　executive〔 ɪg'zɛkjutɪv 〕 *adj*. 執行的

　　　supervise〔,supə'vaɪz〕 *v*. 管理

3. 照會身份保證人

【秘書須知】

- *have given your name as a reference*
  ☞ 提及您作爲身份保證人

- *your opinion of ～* ☞ 您對～意見

- *character and ability* ☞ 品性和能力

- *We assure you that ～* ☞ 我們向您保證～

- *be regarded as strictly confidential*
  ☞ 視爲機密資料；嚴格保密

實　例

October 10, 19 ―

Dear Prof. Lee,

Miss Shu-Fen Chiang applied for a position with our organization as shorthand-typist, and has given your name as a reference.

We should therefore be very grateful if you would let us have your opinion of Miss Chiang's character and ability.

We assure you that any information you may supply will be regarded as strictly confidential.

Yours faithfully,

James Hwang
Personnel Manager

江淑芬小姐應徵我們這個機構，速記員的職位，並且提及您作爲身份保證人。

因此，如果您能讓我們知道，關於您對江小姐品性和能力的意見的話，我們將不勝感激。

我們保證，您所提供的任何資料，將嚴格保密。

✦ ✦ ✦

【註】 organization 〔͵ɔrgənəˈzeʃən〕 *n.* 機構
grateful 〔ˈgretfəl〕 *adj.* 感謝的

4. 保證人的回音

【秘書須知】

* *an outstanding student* ☞ 一個傑出學生
  full of enthusiasm ☞ 充滿熱誠
  full of initiative ☞ 充滿進取的精神

* *show an exceptional talent for ~*
  ☞ 在~方面有特殊才能

* *have all the qualities of a perfect secretary*
  ☞ 具備一個完美秘書的所有才能

* *grant her an interview* ☞ 給她一個面談的機會

───── 實　例 ─────

Dear Mr. Hwang,

I am happy to have the opportunity of answering your letter of October 8.

She was an outstanding student, full of enthusiasm, full of initiative at college, a reporter of the college newspaper and president of the English Speaking Society.

She showed an exceptional talent for typing and writing business letters in English.

I have read some of them and found that she has all the qualities of a perfect secretary as well as shorthand-typist.

I think you will be interested in her and should grant her an interview. I shall be happy to answer any inquiries about Miss Chiang.

Sincerely yours,

....

很高興有機會回覆您10月8日的來信。

在大學時代，她是個傑出的學生，充滿熱誠、進取精神，且是學院報紙的記者，英語演講社社長。

她在打字和英文商業書信方面，表現出特殊才能。

我曾看過一些她的打字和商業書信，發現她具備一個完美秘書及速記員的所有才能。

我想您對她會有興趣，並給她一個面談的機會。我樂意回答有關江小姐的任何查詢。

✦　　　✦　　　✦

【註】 shorthand-typist〔´ʃɔrt͵hænd´taɪpɪst〕*n.* 速記員
inquiry〔ɪn´kwaɪrɪ〕*n.* 查詢，詢問

5. 面談通知函

【 秘書須知 】

- *be pleased to interview you* ☞　　高興與你面談
- *the post advertised* ☞　　廣告刊登的工作

- *above address* ☞　　上述地址

- *mutually convenient appointment* ☞　　彼此方便的約會

- *I confirm that ~* ☞　　我確定~

- *reasonable expenses* ☞　　合理的費用

實　例

Dear Miss Chiang:

　　We shall be pleased to interview you for the post advertised. Would you please call at the company's above address and see our personnel manager, Mr. Hwang at 10:30 a.m. on Tuesday the 14th, May.

　　If the time is impossible for you, would you kindly telephone Miss Chen, secretary to Mr. Hwang, and arrange another mutually convenient appointment.

I confirm that we shall be pleased to pay your fares and other reasonable expenses involved in attending the interview.

Yours Sincerely,

Nancy Chen
Secretary to Mr. Hwang

關於廣告刊登的工作，我們樂意與妳面談。

請在5月14日，星期二上午10點30分，到本公司上述地點，見我們人事經理黃先生。

如果妳不克在那時間前來的話，麻煩妳打電話給黃先生的秘書陳小姐，另外安排彼此方便的約會。

我確定我們會樂於付妳，參加此次面談包括的車馬費，及其他合理的費用。

【註】 fare〔fer〕*n.* 車費
involve〔ɪn'vɑlv〕*v.* 包括
attend〔ə'tend〕*v.* 參加

EXERCISE 1

1.　趙莉莉小姐這次應徵本公司的秘書，以您做為她的身份保證人。

在此，很希望聽聽您對她的人品、家世，以及待人親切、謙恭的能力所提供的意見。

您所提供的任何資料，都將被視為高度機密。

【提示】

- 應徵本公司的秘書
  ☞　*have applied for a position to our company as secretary*

- 提供您做為身份保證人
  ☞　*have given your name as a reference*

- 人品，家世
  ☞　*her personality, her cultural background*

- 待人謙恭、親切的能力
  ☞　*her ability to meet people courteously and graciously*

- 您提供的任何資料將被視為高度機密
  ☞　*Any information you may give us will be treated as strictly confidential.*
  ☞　*Strict confidence will be observed concerning what you may give us.*

2.　　我現在答覆您詢問有關趙莉莉小姐的來函。長期以來，我個人一直非常瞭解她，在她四年大學生活中，我非常關心地看著她成長。

　　她是一個有教養、有學識的女性，在學生時代，她一向是親切而積極的學生，對學校的活動非常熱心。

　　我深信她必能成爲一個值得信賴，而且性情開朗的女秘書。

【提示】

・我個人一直非常了解她
　☞　　**I have known her personally**

・大學四年中☞　　**during her four-year college life**

・我非常關心地看著她成長。
　☞　　**I have followed her progress with much interest**

・有教養、有學問的年輕女性
　☞　　**a young lady of culture and education**

・謙恭且自動自發的學生
　☞　　**be always a courteous and willing student**

・對學校活動很熱心
　☞　　**take keen interest in college activities**

・我深信她會成爲值得信賴和愉快的秘書。
　☞　　**I have every confidence that she will make a reliable and pleasant secretary.**

3. 我剛剛收到您應徵秘書的信函，並很有興趣拜讀過了。

由於本公司擬增加有能力的秘書，所以請您於本週四上午 10 點到 11 點之間，或者下午 3 點至 5 點之間，前來面談。

【提示】

- 收到您應徵秘書的信函。

  ☞ *Your letter applying for a position as secretary has just arrived.*

  ☞ *It was nice of you to write to us thinking of our company as a place where you would like to work as secretary.* （更懇切的說法）

- 擬增加有能力的秘書

  ☞ *plan to increase the number of competent secretaries*

- 上午 10 點至 11 點之間，或者下午 3 點至 5 點之間

  ☞ *either between 10 and 11 a.m. or between 3 and 5 p.m.*

- 前來面談

  ☞ *call for an interview*

4.   經過愼重審議之後,根據我們討論的條件,任用您爲人事主任的
秘書,得便務請從速回覆您的決定,若接受請於19—年8月7日,到
本公司人事主任江一揚先生處報到。

衷心期待您早日成爲我們之間的一員。

【提示】

- 愼重審議之後 ☞   *after careful consideration*

- 根據我們討論的條件
  ☞   *under the terms we discussed*

- 樂意任用您 ～
  ☞   *I am pleased to offer you the post of ～*

- 得便請從速通知您的決定,不勝感激
  ☞   *would appreciate notification of your decision at*
      your earliest convenience

- 請準備向～先生報到
  ☞   *please plan to report to Mr. ～*

- 希望早日成爲我們的一員
  ☞   *look forward to your joining us here soon*

秘書必備常識

秘書的工作廣泛而深入

■　公司的秘書和內閣閣員都稱為 *secretary*

現在的秘書不再祇是同事之間人際關係的潤滑劑或花瓶。Sec-retary＝「秘書」這種公式化的等同，感覺上就覺得缺少了點什麼，其實 secretary 這個字所涵蓋的機能是很廣泛的。Random House 英語辭典對 secretary 的解說是：

secretary [ˈsɛkrətɛrɪ] *n.*, *pl.* -taries.

1. a person, usually an official, who is in charge of the records, correspondence, minutes of meetings, and related affairs of an organization, company, association, etc.: *the secretary of the Linguistic Society of America.*

2. a person employed to handle correspondence and do routine work in a business office, usually involving taking dictation, typing, filing, and the like.

3. See **private secretary**.

4. (*cap.*) an officer of state charged with the superintendence and management of a particular department of government, as a member of the president's cabinet in the U.S.: *Secretary of the Treasury.*

5. a piece of furniture for use as a writing desk.

6. Also called **secretary bookcase**, a desk with bookshelves on top of it.

1. 在機構、公司、或協會等團體中，負責管理檔案、信件、會議紀錄、及相關事務的人，通常是服公職者：如**美國語言學會秘書**。

2. 在商業公司受僱處理信件並執行日常業務，通常包括聽寫、打字、檔案以及同類事務者。

3. 見**私人秘書**

4. （大寫）執掌政府特別部門的監督及管理的國家官員，如美國總統內閣中的一員：**財政部長**

5. 寫字檯。

6. 也稱為（有文件文類函、抽屜的）秘書寫字檯，即其上有書架的桌子。

誠如以上的說明，秘書所從事的工作是非常廣泛深入的。Secretary 這個字本身就有極大的價值感。最近美國的閣員中女性出奇的多。美國對男性閣員稱 Mr. Secretary 或 sir，女性閣員則稱 Madam Secretary。還有些工商團體、福利團體也稱其最高負責人為 Honorary Secretary。因此，Secretary 已從公司的「秘書」，被提昇為政府機構中一個廣為使用的名詞。

■ **在歐美其薪資可比主任**

歐美各國，秘書是令人嚮往的職業，也是公司裏不可缺的一員。高級秘書都擁有一張豪華大辦公桌，薪資可比主任級。歐美企業的行政部門（*executive*）都必須有專屬的能幹女秘書，其工作的表現除了影響上司的績效以外，有時還能左右整個公司的運作。

2) 就任、昇遷、轉任

1. 就任通知函

【秘書須知】

- *be pleased to announce* ～ ☞ 高興宣佈～
- *Chairman of the Board* ☞ 董事會會長
- *President* 〔'prɛzədənt〕 *n.* 董事長，總經理

實 例

Dear Sirs，

We are pleased to announce the election of Mr. Ta-hwa Wang as Chairman of the Board and Mr. Ming-shan Chen as President.

Sheng Sheng Trading Co., Ltd.

August 10th, 19—

我們樂於宣佈，王大華先生當選董事會會長，陳明山先生當選總經理。

✦ ✦ ✦

【註】 election〔ɪ'lɛkʃən〕*n.* 選舉

2. 祝賀總經理就任

【秘書須知】

- *able leadership* ☞ 能幹的領導
- *grow and prosper* ☞ 成長、興隆
- *in the years to come* ☞ 將來

實 例

Dear Mr. Chen,

I have just learned from Mr. Wu that you have been elected president of your company. Please accept our sincere congratulations. I am sure you must be very happy on this honor and under your able leadership your company will grow and prosper in the years to come.

Yours Sincerely,

Rebert Chiang
President

我剛從吳先生處獲悉,你被選爲貴公司總經理。請接受我們誠摯祝賀之意。我確信你一定以這份榮耀爲樂,而在你能幹的領導下,貴公司將會成長、興隆。

【註】 sincere〔sɪn'sɪr〕*adj.* 誠摯的
accept〔ək'sɛpt〕*v.* 接受

3. 受祝賀者回覆

【秘書須知】

- ***justify the confidence shown in me***
  ☞ 　不辜負對我的信心
- ***associate*** 〔 ə'soʃɪɪt 〕 *n.* 同事；同僚

實　例

Dear Mr. Chiang,

　　Thank you very much for your letter congratulating me on my election as president of this company.

　　I shall certainly do my best to justify the confidence shown in me by my associates.

Cordially Yours,

Ming-shan Chen

President

很感激你來信，祝賀我當選敝公司總經理。

我定會竭盡所能，不辜負同事們對我的信心。

【註】　congratulate〔kən'grætʃə,let〕*v.* 祝賀
　　　　cordially〔'kɔrdʒəlɪ〕*adv.* 誠懇地

4. 祝賀就任分公司經理

【秘書須知】

- *Manager of your Taipei Office* ☞ 台北公司的經理

- *hasten to* ☞ 急於；匆忙

- *my colleagues and I* ☞ 同事與我

- *full cooperation* ☞ 全面合作

- *at all times* ☞ 隨時

實 例

Dear Mr. Wu,

The good news of your appointment as Manager of your Taipei Office has just reached me and I hasten to wish you the best of success and happiness in your new post. My colleagues and I welcome you to Taipei and assure you of our full cooperation at all times.

Cordially yours,

John Lee

Manager of Overseas Division

　　我剛得知您就任台北公司經理的好消息。匆此祝福您在新的任內勝任愉快。同事和我歡迎您到台北，並向您保證我們隨時與您全力合作。

【註】　appointment〔əˈpɔɪntmənt〕*n.* 職位；任用；委派
　　　　success〔səkˈsɛs〕*n.* 成就，成功
　　　　assure〔əˈʃʊr〕*v.* 保證

5. 祝賀新任董事

【秘書須知】

- *new appointment to the Board* ☞　董事會的新職位
- *(offer) our very best wishes for the future*
　☞　祝福未來

實　例

Dear Mr. Lin,

　　I am delighted to hear of your new appointment to the Board. The many years you have worked with the Company have been rewarded, and my partner and I offer you our warmest congratulations and our very best wishes for the future.

Sincerely yours,

....

President

🖥 我樂於聽到你在董事會的新職位。你在公司工作多年，已得到酬報，我和我的夥伴向你致最熱誠的祝賀之意，並祝福你的未來。

【註】 delighted〔dɪ'laɪtɪd〕 *adj.* 欣喜的；高興的
reward〔rɪ'wɔrd〕 *v.* 報酬

6. 就任新職時的通知

【秘書須知】

- *It is my pleasure to inform you that ~*
  ☞ 很高興通知你~

- *be appointed ~* ☞ 被任命為~

- *Head Office* ☞ 總公司

- *Deputy Manager* ☞ 副經理

- *take over the managership of ~* ☞ 接管~之職權

- *as from September 16* ☞ 自9月16日起

- *the assistance and kindness you have given (=rendered) me in the past*
  ☞ 你們以往一直給予我的協助和親切

- *In this connection* ☞ 關於這點

實 例

Dear Sirs,

　　It is my pleasure to inform you that I have been appointed Manager of our Overseas Division at the Head Office and Mr. Billy Wang, who has been Deputy

Manager of Sales Division, will take over the managership of this office as from September 16, 19—

I should like to thank you for the assistance and kindness you have given me in the past.

In this connection, I trust you will kindly extend Mr. Wang the same courtesy and cooperation as you have given me.

With warmest personal regards,

Yours sincerely,

....

很高興通知各位，我已被任命爲總公司的海外部經理。自19—，9月16日起，銷售部副經理王比利先生將接管這個公司的職權。

感激你們以往一直給予我的協助和親切。

關於這點，我相信你們會像過去對我一樣，親切地給予王先生同樣的禮遇和合作。

敬致個人最熱誠的問候之意。

【註】 Overseas Division 海外部
Sales Division 銷售部
managership〔'mænɪdʒə,ʃɪp〕n. 經理的職位或權力
extend〔ɪk'stɛnd〕v. 給予
courtesy〔'kɜtəsɪ〕n. 禮遇；謙恭的行爲；殷勤
with best (kind) regards 敬致問候之意

7. 祝賀新任經理

【秘書須知】

- *It is with great pleasure that ~* ☞ 很高興~
- *my fellow directors and myself*
  ☞ 董事會同事和我本人
- *looking back on* ☞ 回顧
- *excellent activities in the past* ☞ 以往卓越的活動

實 例

Dear Mr. Yu,

It is with great pleasure that my fellow directors and myself heard of your being appointed Manager of the Overseas Division.

Looking back on your excellent activities in the past, I know that your enthusiasm and experience are the very qualities needed for this position.

My colleagues join me in offering you our warmest congratulations and best wishes for the future.

With kindest regards,

Yours truly,

....

Manager of Sales Division

董事會同事和我本人，很高興聽到你被任命爲海外部經理。

回顧你以往的卓越的活動，我知道你的熱心和經驗，正是這職位所需要的才能。

同事們和我，對你獻上我們最熱誠的祝賀，並祝福你的未來。

謹致最親切的問候之意

✦　　　　✦　　　　✦

【註】　enthusiasm〔ɪnˈθjuzɪˌæzəm〕*n.* 熱心
　　　quality〔ˈkwɑlətɪ〕*n.* (*pl.*) 才能
　　　colleague〔ˈkɑlig〕*n.* 同事

8。駐任人員替換的通知

【秘書須知】

- *our representative in Taichung*
  ☞ 我們駐台中的代表

- *have been transferred to the Head Office*
  ☞ 調往總公司

- *manager of Chemical Department* ☞ 化學部經理

- *be assigned to = be appointed to* ☞ 被指派

- *succeeding Mr. Lee* ☞ 繼任李先生的職位

- *I should be much obliged if~*
  ☞ 如果~，我將不勝感激

- *the courtesy and help which you kindly extended to his predecessor, Mr. Lee*
  ☞ 給予殷勤協助，一如你親切地對前任的李先生 樣。

實 例

April 5, 19 —

Dear Sir,

I am pleased to inform you that Mr. Lee, our representative in Taichung, has been transferred to the Head Office and Mr. Lin, who has been the manager of the Chemical Department, is now assigned to that post succeeding Mr. Lee.

I should be much obliged if you would give him the courtesy and help which you kindly extended to his predecessor, Mr. Lee.

Yours sincerely,

．．．．．．．．．．．．．．．．．

Personnel Manager

我樂於通知你，我們駐台中的代表李先生，已被調往總公司，而化學部經理林先生，已被指派繼任李先生的職位。

如果你能給予他殷勤協助，一如你親切地對前任的李先生一樣，我將不勝感激。

✦　　　✦　　　✦

【註】　inform〔ɪnˈfɔrm〕v. 通知
predecessor〔ˌprɛdɪˈsɛsə〕n. 前任者

EXERCISE 2

1.　　我收到您當選爲貴公司董事長的通知，眞是爲您高興。我和熟識
您的茂源公司職員們，共同爲您的昇遷而感到高興。我和同事們一同
祈願，您在今後的事業和健康上都有不凡的進展。

　　今後，我們會一本以往，同樣地支持、幫助您，請勿掛念。祝今
後一切安好。

【提示】

- 獲知～非常高興　☞　　*be extremely pleased to learn of ～*

- 我和同事們都祈願您～

　　☞　　*They joined me in wishing you ～*

- 請安心　☞　　*please be assured of ～*

- 一本以往的支持與協助

　　☞　　*continued patronage and cooperation*

- 祝今後一切安好　☞　　（可直接譯爲）*with best wishes*

2.　　在此通知您一聲，由於國際貿易公司西雅圖辦事處主任陳東智先
生退休，所以任命江輝龍先生接替，希望您能像對前任的陳先生一樣，
給予他鼓勵和協助。

【提示】

- 任命江輝龍先生爲～

　　☞　　*Hui-lung Chiang has been named ～*

- 接替離職的陳東智先生
     replacing Tung-chin Chen who resigned

- 像對前任者一樣,給予他鼓勵和協助
     give him the courtesy and help which you kindly
     extended to his predecessor, Mr. Chen

3.　特爲知會,本人這次被任爲陽光貿易股份有限公司董事長。

【提示】

- 特爲知會～。
     It is my pleasure to inform you that ～.
     It is with great pleasure that ～.

4.　衷心恭賀您就任貴公司紐約分處的負責人。

【提示】

- 您就任～
     your recent appointment to the post of ～

- 由衷恭賀您～
     offer you our hearty congratulations on ～

學英文的書 , 學習都有

秘書必備常識

期待歐美型的秘書出現

■ 任用有能力的秘書使業績躍昇的實例

這是台灣一家超級企業公司的眞實事例。那家公司本來在歐洲的銷售的業績一直欲振乏力，因此有人主張採用一位有能力的女秘書，並呈請人事主任採高薪制聘請了一位能力過人的女秘書。

這位女秘書有著令人刮目相看的能力和遠見，總能適時給予經理適切的建議，在短時間內銷售量倍增，很快就達到了三年計畫的目標。

反觀國內一般的秘書地位又是如何呢？現在雖正當「辦公室自動化」的事務革命期間，然而卻仍有許多公司需要秘書在辦公室內扮演人際潤滑的工作。國內各大企業的主管們莫不期望著歐美型秘書的早日出現。

歐美型秘書大致分爲五種階層，除接待員 **Receptionist** 以外，還有其他四種：

Secretary Typist	附屬於一位或數位主管，以速記或打字爲主要工作。
Junior Secretary	卽助理秘書，輔佐主要秘書，是成爲高級秘書的過渡型。
Private Secretary (Confidential Secretary)	是經理、主任級的 man-to-man 秘書，可委之以部分重要工作，對工作需要有高度的了解和判斷力。
Executive Secretary	隸屬於總負責人或主管；有極大的權力，並須有高度的知識、能力、判斷力及豐富的經驗。因此這個階層的秘書不是年輕女性所能勝任的，大多是經驗豐富，年齡較大的小姐或女士居於其位。

3) 介 紹 信

1。介紹生意上有來往的對象

【秘書須知】

- *It gives us great pleasure to introduce to you by this letter Mr. ~ = I am writing this letter for Mr. ~*
  ☞ 很榮幸藉這封信爲你介紹 ～ 先生。

- *have done business for many years*
  ☞ 做生意多年

- *to extend the sales organization* ☞ 擴展銷售組織

- *if you would give him your advice and experience*
  ☞ 如果你願提供他忠告和經驗

實 例

Dear Mr. Nelson,

It gives us great pleasure to introduce to you by this letter Mr. Ta-kwang Yang, manager of the Overseas Division of Central Motor Company, Ltd., with whom we have done business for many years. Mr. Yang will be visiting Canada in the near future to extend the Cen-

[圖] 4. 模範秘書英語書信 *79*

tral sales organization. We should consider it a great

favor if you would give him your advice and experience.

Yours sincerely,

....

Manager, Marketing Div.

很高興藉這封信為你介紹，中央馬達有限公司海外部經理，楊大光先生，他與我們做生意多年。最近楊先生將訪問加拿大以擴展中央公司的銷售組織。我們認為如果你願提供他忠告和經驗，將是一大助益。

【註】　extend 〔 ɪkˈstɛnd 〕v. 擴展　　consider 〔 kənˈsɪdɚ 〕v. 認為
　　　　favor 〔 ˈfevɚ 〕n. 幫助

2. 介紹分公司新任負責人

【秘書須知】

- *This will serve to introduce ~* ☞ 這是為了介紹~

- *have a long business history of ~*
  ☞ 有~的悠久商業經歷

- *electric appliances* ☞ 家庭電化製品（家電）

- *is planning to go to Los Angeles*
  ☞ 正計劃前往洛杉磯

- *with the purpose of setting up their new office*
  ☞ 目的是設立新辦事處

- *Your full cooperation in this matter would be appreciated.*
  ☞ 你對這件事的全力合作，將令我們十分感激。

實　例

Dear Mr. Smith,

　　This will serve to introduce Mr. Ta-Ming Liu,

president of China Electric Corporation who has a long

business history of exporting electric appliances to the

United States. Mr. Lin is planning to go to Los

Angeles with the purpose of setting up their new office

there to cover the territory of California. Your full
cooperation in this matter would be very much appreciated.

Sincerely yours,

....

President

　　這封信是爲了介紹中國電器公司總經理，劉大明先生。對於出口
家電製品到美國，他有悠久的商業經歷。劉先生正計劃前往洛杉磯，
目的是設立一個涵蓋加州地區的新辦事處。你對這件事的全力合作，
將令我們十分感激。

✦　　　　✦　　　　✦

【註】　export (ɪks'port) *v.* 出口
　　　　territory 〔 'tɛrəˌtorɪ 〕 *n.* 區域

3. 介紹新的事業夥伴

【秘書須知】

- *have great pleasure in introducing to you*

  ☞ 很高興爲你介紹

- *business associate* ☞ 事業夥伴

- *establish new connections* ☞ 建立新的業務關係

實 例

Dear Mr. Yang,

We have great pleasure in introducing to you, by this letter, Mr. Kenneth Green, President of Gulf & Western Corporation, New York, who is our business associate.

Mr. Green is visiting Taipei to establish new connections and we should greatly appreciate any assistance you may be able to give him.

Yours sincerely,

....

Executive Vice-President

很高興藉此信為你介紹我們的事業夥伴,紐約西方海灣公司總經理肯尼斯‧格林先生。

格林先生正訪問台北以建立新的業務關係,如果你能給他任何協助,我們將非常感激。

✦　　　✦　　　✦

【註】　gulf〔gʌlf〕*n.* 海灣
assistance〔əˈsɪstəns〕*n.* 協助

4. 上司出差必須會見某人

【秘書須知】

· ***I wonder if ~*** ☞　　我想知道～；我是否～

⇒ I *wonder if* you'd look after my daughter while I go shopping.　我想知道我購物時，你能否看顧我的女兒。

⇒ I *wonder if*（whether）I might ask you a question.
　我是否可以問你一個問題。

實　例

Dear Mr. Liu

　　I am writing this letter for Henry Smith who plans to be in Taipei for about a month. Mr. Smith is the manager of Far East Sales Divison of Sunlight Golf Equipment Corporation in New York. He would very much like to meet you on the morning of, say, 10th or 11th May and wonders if one of those days would be

[圖] 4. 模範秘書英語書信　*85*

convenient. As he is leaving for his trip pretty soon,

we should be most grateful to have your reply as soon

as possible.

Yours sincerely,

Mary Hwang
Secretary to Mr. Martell

　　　我替亨利・史密斯先生寫這封信，他計劃到台北一個月左右。史密斯先生是紐約陽光高爾夫裝備公司的遠東銷售部主任，他很希望在5月10日或11日早上與你見面，並想知道那天較爲方便。因爲他很快就要啓程，儘早收到你的答覆，我們將感激萬分。

✦　　　✦　　　✦

【註】　equipment〔ɪˈkwɪpmənt〕*n.* 裝備
　　　　grateful〔ˈgretfəl〕*adj.* 感激的
　　　　reply〔rɪˈplaɪ〕*n.* 答覆

EXERCISE 3

1.　　我要介紹這封信的持有人江隆清先生。他是台北大大電器貿易股
　　份有限公司的出口部經理，這家公司是台灣衆多製造各種袖珍型電子
　　計算機的一流廠商之一。

【提示】

· 出口部經理 ☞　　　***Export Manager***

· 各種袖珍型電子計算機
　　☞　　***various types of pocket-size Electronic Calcula-***
　　　　　tors

· 一流廠商之一
　　☞　　***one of the top-ranking manufacturers***

2.　　我們很高興爲您介紹這封信的持有人─興田化學股份有限公司常
　　務董事何三木先生。他預定在5月5日抵達貴市，預定在5月5日到
　　5月20日之間停留貴寶地。他這次出差的目的是要和加州地區的主
　　要纖維產品進口商接觸。停留期間，幸祈各位能親切地協助並鼓勵他。

【提示】

· 我們很高興爲您介紹～。
　　☞　　***It gives us great pleasure to introduce to you～.***

· 這封信的持有者
　　☞　　***the bearer of this letter***

- 常務董事 ☞　*executive director*
  ☞　*managing director*
- 預定 ☞　*be scheduled to*
- 和主要紡織產品進口商接觸
  ☞　*to contact some leading textiles importers*
- 若您能～，我們將非常感激。
  ☞　*We would greatly appreciate it if you could ～.*
- 親切的幫助和禮遇
  ☞　*kind assistance and courtesies*

3.　尼爾森先生：

　　我現在爲您介紹新任銷售部長陳川弘先生。陳先生繼任上週退休的江隆茂先生。陳先生最近要出差前往舊金山分公司和您見面，並聽聽舊金山地區的銷售計畫。你將會感受到他對每一件事情的熱誠。

　　陳先生很快就會啟程，他的秘書會以電話或信件和您聯絡，請您去迎接他，並簡報舊金山地區的營業狀況。

【提示】

- 他繼任～。☞　*He is succeeding ～.*
- 最近要出差到舊金山分公司
  ☞　*will soon be visiting our San Francisco branch*
- 你將會感受到他對任何事情的熱誠。
  ☞　*You'll enjoy his enthusiastic approach to everything he does.*

- 他的秘書會以電話或信件和你聯絡
  - ☞ *You can expect a call or letter from his secretary.*

- 簡報營業狀況
  - ☞ *brief him on your operation*

秘書必備常識

秘書是使介紹積極進行的重要人物

■　不要把介紹的順序搞錯

介紹是秘書的一項重要工作，在宴會及會議的場合，若是不明白介紹的方法，不但會貽笑大方，而且很可能會招來誤會，而影響到整個會場的順利和成功。

我國的大型招待會或者宴會上，若有數人在攀談，席間出現一個大家所不熟悉的人，通常是不加以介紹的。但在歐美，若有這種情形發生，會令當事人感到自己無足輕重或受到輕視。此外，在介紹時不要搞錯順序，否則會給別人不愉快的感受。

秘書絕不是宴席，會場中的壁花，為上司引見訪客，積極地為來賓互相介紹，成為一項極為重要的職務。

■　向地位高者介紹他人

介紹時必須考慮身份地位，習慣上是將地位低的人向地位高的人介紹。首先說出地位高的人的名字，以引起大家注意，然後再依序介紹其他人的姓名，例如，妳要為陳董事長大人介紹小公司的職員時：

Mrs. Chen, let me introduce Mr. Chao (to you).

更輕鬆融洽的介紹可用：

Mrs. Chen, this is Mr. Chao.

若是同時介紹兩、三個人的時候，Let me introduce you to Mr. ～似嫌太過繁瑣，可較簡明地說：

Mrs. Chen,（呼吸）, Mr. Chao. Mr. Chiang. Mr. Lai.

下面再舉出一個介紹時的實況會話：

1. Mr. Smith, this is Mr. Chiang, our Overseas Manager. Mr. Chiang, this is Mr. Smith, President of Sunlight Chemical Corporation.

   史密斯先生，這位是江先生，本公司的海外部 經理。
   江先生，這位是史密斯先生，陽光化學公司的董事長。

2. How do you do, Mr. Smith？I am pleased to meet you.

   史密斯先生，您好，我很高興認識您。

3. How do you do, Mr. Chiang？I am glad to meet you, too.

   江先生，您好，我也很高興認識您。

4) 聯繫與謝意

1. 詳稟會面事宜與敲定時間

【秘書須知】

- ***research and development manager*** ☞　研究開發部經理

- ***represent*** 〔ˌrɛprɪ'zɛnt〕*v*. 代表

- ***travel*** 〔'trævl̩〕*v*. 〔商業〕出外拜訪；出外徵求訂貨；出外推銷

實　例

6th January, 19—

Dear Mr. Stone,

　　Mr. Chung-hwa Wang, our research and development manager, will be spending two weeks in Canada shortly on business. He represents a large Taiwan pharmaceutical company, Chengkwang of Taiwan. Most of his time will be spent traveling to our suppliers, agents and customers in Canada.

　　He would welcome the opportunity of seeing you while he is in Ottawa.

　　Mr. Wang would like to meet either yourself or an experienced person in your Chemical or Pharmaceutical Division.

He will be in Ottawa on the 16th, 17th and 18th of January inclusive.

I would be grateful if you could fix an appointment. The time of day is unimportant.

Yours faithfully,

....

Secretary

我們的研究開發部經理，王中華先生，近期內因公前往加拿大兩週。他代表台灣一家大規模製藥公司，台灣正光。他將花大部分時間四處拜訪我們加拿大供應商、代理商及顧客。

他在渥太華時，歡迎有機會與你見面。

王先生希望和你本人或化學部、製藥部的一位有經驗人士見面。1月16、17、18日三天，他會在渥太華。

如果你能確定會面時間，則感幸甚。

哪一天見面都沒有關係。

✦   ✦   ✦

【註】 pharmaceutical〔ˌfɑrməˈsjutɪkḷ〕*adj.* 製藥的
supplier〔səˈplaɪɚ〕*n.* 供應者　　agent〔ˈedʒənt〕*n.* 代理人
inclusive〔ɪnˈklusɪv〕*adj.* 包括的　　fix〔fɪks〕*v.* 確定；決定

2. 回覆會面信函

【秘書須知】

* *request an appointment* ☞ 要求約定會面時間
* *Head Office in Ottawa* ☞ 渥太華的總公司。
* *Senior Research Officer* ☞ 高級研究員
* *ask for Mr. Smith's secretary* ☞ 找史密斯先生的秘書
* *please do not hesitate to ~* ☞ 請別猶豫~

實　例

Dear Miss White,

Thank you for your letter of the 6th, in which you requested an appointment. Mr. Smith will be pleased to receive a visit from Mr. Wang, Tuesday, the 17th of January at 11:00 a.m. at our Head Office in Ottawa. He is a Senior Research Officer in our Chemical Division.

When Mr. Wang arrives, please ask for Mr. Smith's secretary. I trust this date and time is convenient.

If it is not, please do not hesitate to telephone.

Yours faithfully,

Rebecca Chao
Secretary to Mr. Smith

感謝妳6日來信，要求約定會面時間。史密斯先生很高興於1月17日，星期二早上11點，在渥太華的總公司，與王先生會晤。他是我們化學部高級研究員。

王先生抵達時，請找史密斯先生的秘書。

我相信這日期與時間是方便的。

如果不方便，請別猶豫來電告知。

【註】 convenient 〔kən'vinjənt〕 *adj.* 方便的；適宜的

3. 與上司欲訪問的企業聯繫

【秘書須知】

· *accompanied by Mr. ～* ☞　由～先生陪同

· *Assistant Manager of the same Department*
　☞　同一部門的副理

· *your associates* ☞　同事

· *Messrs. = Messieurs* 〔ˈmɛsəz〕*n.(pl.)*
　〔法文〕先生的複數形；諸位先生；諸君

· *will be of mutual benefit to our two companies*
　☞　對我們兩家公司都有利

實　例

Dear Mr. Stockton,

　　We are pleased to inform you that our Mr. Chung-
ming Wu, Manager of Foreign Department, accompanied
by Mr. Ta-shan Wang, Assistant Manager of the same
Department, is scheduled to arrive at your city on
May 3rd for a business trip. This will be the first
visit to your city for both Mr. Wu and Wang and they
look forward to meeting you and your associates. We

believe that the discussions by Messrs. Wu and Wang

with you will be of mutual benefit to our two compa-

nies. Any advice and counsel you will give them will be

very much appreciated by all of us.

Sincerely yours,

Nancy Lee

Secretary

很高興通知你，我們國外部經理吳中民先生，在該部副經理王大山先生的陪同下，因公事旅行，預定在5月3日抵達貴城市。這是吳先生和王先生兩位第一次到貴城市訪問，他們期望和你及你的同事會晤。我們相信你和吳、王兩位先生之間的討論，對我們兩家公司都有利。任何你給予他們的忠告和建議，將令我們不勝感激。

◆　　　◆　　　◆

【註】　schedule〔ˈskɛdʒʊl〕 *v.* 預定；安排
　　　mutual〔ˈmjutʃʊəl〕 *adj.* 相互的；共同的
　　　counsel〔ˈkaʊnsl̩〕 *n.* 建議

4. 對於訪問期間的照顧表示謝意

【秘書須知】

* *before settling down to the normal routine again*

  ☞　在尚未安定下來，專心於日常工作之前

* *take this opportunity to～* ☞　藉此機會～

* *kind reception and assistance* ☞　親切款待與協助

* *Head Office* ☞　總辦事處；總公司

* *your Directors* ☞　董事們

* *should there be any matters in which you think I may be able to be of some assistance*

  ☞　如果有任何事你認為我可以幫得上忙

實　例

Dear Mr. Stockton,

On Sunday last Mr. Wang and I returned to Taiwan and, before settling down to the normal routine again, I would like to take this opportunity to express our sincere thanks for the kind reception and assistance you have given us during our stay in your city.

Your warm welcome at your Head Office and the happy evenings spent with you and your Directors in San Francisco are very much in my memory. Do not hesitate to write me, should there be any matters in which you think I may be able to be of some assistance. I hope you will pay a visit to Taiwan at the earliest opportunity.

Sincerely yours,

Chung-ming Wu

Manager, Foreign Dept.

王先生和我於上週日返回台灣，在尚未安定下來，專心於日常業務之前，我願藉此機會，為我們在貴市停留期間，你所給予的親切款待和協助，表達我們誠摯的謝意。

你在貴總辦事處熱烈歡迎我們，以及在舊金山與你和貴董事們共度的愉快夜晚，令我記憶良深。如果有任何事你認為我可以幫得上忙，別猶豫，來信告知。希望你儘快有機會到台灣一遊。

✦　　　　✦　　　　✦

【註】　reception〔rɪ'sɛpʃən〕*n*. 接待
　　　　assistance〔ə'sɪstəns〕*n*. 協助

EXERCISE 4

1.　敬啟者：

　　我是東京陽光體育用品股份有限公司的職員，預定於今年10月15日星期一至10月19日星期五之間，到紐約訪問，拜訪您並討論敝公司最近所開發的高爾夫球鞋。

　　10月17日星期三上午9點30分方便嗎？

　　要是日期、時間不方便，請指示其他的時間、日期，麻煩您回信告知。

　　　　　　　　　　　　　　　　　　專此

　　　　　　　高　眞　昌
　　　　　　　營業經理

【提示】

・ 我是陽光體育用品股份有限公司的職員。
　☞　*I come（am）from Sunlight Sports Goods Company Limited.*

・ 10月15日星期一到10月19日星期五之間
　☞　*from Monday, October 15 to Friday, October 19*

・ 討論敝公司新開發的高爾夫球鞋
　☞　*discuss our newly-developed golf shoes*

・ 若是這日期、時間不方便
　☞　*if the date or the time is not convenient*

・ 請指示其他的日期、時間。☞　*Please suggest another.*

2. 高先生：

　　謝謝您 10 月 4 日的來信。我想見您並討論貴公司新開發的高
爾夫球鞋產品，可惜星期三上午 9 點 30 分恐怕沒辦法，18 日星期
四上午 9 點 30 分可以會晤，希望這個時間對您方便。期待您的到
來。

【提示】

- 恐怕我無法～。
  ☞ *I am afraid I cannot manage～.*

- 我希望這個時間對您方便。
  ☞ *I hope this will be convenient for you.*

3. 　　謝謝您知會陳先生要來此拜訪的事。福特先生很樂意見他，您提
出的拜訪日期，星期一上午 10 點 30 分對福特先生很方便。

【提示】

- 您來函知會～
  ☞ *Your letter informing me that Mr. Chen will be visiting～*

- 福特先生很樂意見他。
  ☞ *Mr. Ford will be pleased to meet him.*

- （您）提出的拜訪日期
  ☞ *the proposed date of call*

4.　　謝謝您告知江先生將蒞臨底特律的來信。但不巧福特先生目前正短期出差到加拿大，9月20日才會回來。因此，若江先生9月20日之後到底特律的話，福特先生很樂意和他會面。

若可能，請速回函告知。

【提示】

- 不巧 ☞　**unfortunately**（不可用 I am sorry, 或者 It is quite regrettable）

- 如果他能在9月20日之後來底特律的話
  ☞　**if he could be in Detroit after 20th September**
  （因前面已有 20th September, 故此處亦可用 after that date）

5.　　上次到紐約短期出差，承蒙您無微不至的幫助，又提供有用的資料，眞是非常感謝。托您的福，這是一次非常愉快而收穫良多的出差。誠如我前幾天所說的，希望藉著邀請您到台灣來，接受敝公司的招待作爲回報，希望您把行程留一天給敝公司，讓我爲您介紹台北。

我期待著在台北會晤的那一天。

【提示】

- 您所提供的親切協助及有用的資料
  ☞　**for the kind help and useful information you gave me**

- 上次的紐約短期出差
  ☞　**on my last short business trip to New York**

- 非常愉快而收穫良多的旅行
  - ☞ *a very enjoyable as well as fruitful trip*

- 如我前幾天提到的
  - ☞ *as I mentioned the other day*

- 藉著邀請您到台灣來,回報您殷勤的招待
  - ☞ *to return your hospitality by inviting you to Taiwan*

- 留一天的行程給我們
  - ☞ *leave one day of your schedule to us*

- 我建議~ ☞ *Let me suggest ~*

秘書必備常識

接到外國人的電話怎麼辦?

聽一個公司職員、秘書接電話,大概就可以知道這個公司職員的教育水準。

不論男、女職員,聽到電話鈴聲響,能夠非常安詳地拿起話筒,重點式的應對,才不愧是稱職的職員。由於近來與國外交易日漸頻繁,在商業機構,如果不能以極自然從容的態度應對國內、外電話,也稱不上是公司稱職的一員。以下是接聽電話的應對方法:

■　聽不清對方姓名時，應再確認對方姓名

・ I am sorry, I couldn't catch you.

・ May I have your name, again, please?

■　接聽電話時

聽到對方說 Could you get me 567?（內線電話）或者 Give me Extention 567，或單單是 Extention 567 時，最好回答 Just a moment, please.

若為指名電話則應回答 Just a minute, please. 然後接著說：

・ Thank you for waiting. Mr. Chen is on the line.

（謝謝您等候，陳先生來了。）

若當事人出差或正在開會，則可回答：

・ Mr. Chen is at a meeting（in conference）right now.

（陳先生正在開會。）

・ Mr. Chen is not at his desk now.

（陳先生現在不在。）

・ Mr. Chen has just stepped out.

（陳先生剛出去。）

・ Would you like to leave a message?

（你要留話嗎？）

找人代替接聽時則說：

・ I have Mr. Chiang for you. He is on the line now. Please go ahead.

（我請江先生代聽，他來了，請說。）

5) 出差、視察的行程表

1. 出差旅行的行程

【秘書須知】

· *itinerary* 〔 aɪˈtɪnəˌrɛrɪ 〕 *n.* 旅程，日程

· *All the Branch Managers' Roundtable*（*Conference*）
☞ 所有分公司經理的會議

· *pick you up at ~* ☞ 在~接你；到~載你

· *branch offices* ☞ 支店；分公司

· *facts and statistics on plant operations*
☞ 工廠經營的現狀與統計資料

· *foreman* 〔ˈformən〕 *n.* 工頭；領班

· *staff canteen* ☞ 員工餐飲部

· *executive staff* ☞ 全體行政人員

實 例

Mr. Blackwell's Itinerary in Japan

Tokyo — Nagoya — Osaka — Hiroshima — Tokyo

Monday, March 5（Tokyo Head Office）
   9:30 a.m.   All the Branch Managers' Roundtable
                       （File No. 1 in your briefcase for this
                       occasion）

| 1:00 p.m. | All the Sales Managers' Roundtable (File No. 2) |

| 6:00 p.m. | Company dinner at Hotel Hilton (File No. 3 contains a copy of the Speech for this occasion) |

Tuesday, March 6 (Tokyo to Nagoya)

| 10:00 a.m. | Bill Yeh, Manager at Tokyo, will pick you up at Hotel Hilton and drive you to Haneda Airport. |

| 11:50 a.m. | Leave Haneda Airport on Japan Airline Flight No. 75 (First class, Luncheon) |

| 1:00 p.m. | Arrive Nagoya. Stay at Hotel New Nagoya (Double room with bath booked) Tommy Chen, Office Manager at Nagoya branch, will pick you up at the airport and take you to the Hotel. |

| 3:00 p.m. | Conference scheduled at branch offices. (File No. 4) |

| 5:00 p.m. | Company dinner will be held at Hotel New Nagoya. (File No. 4 — Copy of the speech) |

Wednesday, March 7 (Nagoya to Osaka)

9:00 a.m. Tommy Chen will pick you up at the hotel and drive you to Nagoya Station. (J.N.R.)

9:30 a.m. Leave Nagoya by Shinkansen Line. (bullet train)

10:30 p.m. Arrive Osaka, Jimmy Lin, Office Manager, will pick you up at the station and take you to the Royal Hotel. Have luncheon at the hotel.

1:00 p.m. You are to inspect the New Osaka Plant this afternoon. (File No. 6 contains facts and statistics on plant operations)

4:00 p.m. Conference scheduled at the plant conference room. Production manager and all the foremen will attend.

6:00 p.m. Dinner meeting at the staff canteen will follow.

Thursday, March 8 (Osaka to Hiroshima)

9:30 a.m. Billy Lee will pick you up to take you to the station. (J.N.R.)

10:00 a.m. Leave Osaka by Shinkansen Line.

[图] 4. 模範秘書英語書信　*107*

12:00 p.m.　　　　Arrive Hiroshima.

John Wu, Office Manager, will meet you at the station and drive you to Hotel Hiroshima. Have dinner at the hotel.

2:00 p.m.　　　　Visit Hiroshima Offices.

Conference scheduled at the conference room. (File No. 6 contains statistics and report of progress of this branch)

6:00 p.m.　　　　Company dinner. Diamond Restaurant of Hotel Hiroshima. (Copy of the Speech in File No. 7).

Friday, March 9　(Hiroshima)

　Free day.

10:00 a.m.　　　Leave the Hotel for sightseeing.

12:00 p.m　　　　Have lunch at Hiroshima Country Club.

1:00 p.m.　　　　Golf with Mr. and Mrs. Wu.

6:00 p.m.　　　　Dinner Appointment at Wu's home. (Telephone 51-0731)

Saturday, March 10 (Hiroshima — Tokyo)

10:00 a.m.　　　John Wu will pick you up to take you to the station. (J.N.R.)

10:30 a.m.	Leave Hiroshima by Shinkansen for Tokyo.
2:30 p.m.	Arrive Tokyo.
	Mr. Yu, manager of administration will meet you at the station and drive you to the Tokyo Head Office.
4:00 p.m.	Conference with executive staff at the Head Office. (File No. 8)
6:00 p.m.	Company dinner with executive staff at Hotel President. (Double room with bath booked)
Sunday, March 11	(Tokyo — Taipei)
9:30 a.m.	Tom Chao, General Manager, will pick you up at the hotel and take you to Narita International Airport.
11:30 a.m.	Check in at air terminal.
12:30 p.m.	Departure.
	Cathay Pacific Airways Flight No. 115. (First class, Luncheon)

布拉克威爾先生的日本行程

東京—名古屋—大阪—廣島—東京

3月5日，星期一　（東京總公司）

　　早上9:30　　　所有分公司經理的會議

　　　　　　　　　（這個場合需用的1號檔案在你的公事包裏）

　　下午1:00　　　所有銷售部經理的會議

　　　　　　　　　（2號檔案）

　　下午6:00　　　在希爾頓飯店，公司聚餐

　　　　　　　　　（3號檔案有這個場合的演講稿）

3月6日星期二　　（東京到名古屋）

　　早上10:00　　東京經理葉畢爾，將到希爾頓飯店接你，

　　　　　　　　　載你到羽田機場。

　　早上11:50　　搭乘75班次日航班機（頭等艙，供應午餐）

　　　　　　　　　離開羽田機場。

　　下午1:00　　　抵達名古屋。

　　　　　　　　　住新名古屋飯店

　　　　　　　　　（訂好一間雙人套房）

　　　　　　　　　名古屋分公司的經理，陳湯米將到機場接

　　　　　　　　　你，送你到飯店。

　　下午3:00　　　預定在分公司開會。

　　　　　　　　　（4號檔案）

　　下午5:00　　　在新名屋飯店舉行公司聚餐。

　　　　　　　　　（4號檔案—演講稿）

3月7日，星期三　　（從名古屋到大阪）

早上9:00　　　　陳湯米將到飯店接你，載你到名古屋火車站。（日本國營鐵路）

早上9:30　　　　搭新幹線離開名古屋。

（子彈列車）

早上10:30　　　抵達大阪。公司經理林吉米，將到火車站接你，送你到國王飯店。

在飯店吃午餐。

早上1:00　　　　這一天下午，你將視察新大阪工廠

（6號檔案有工廠經營現狀與統計資料）

下午4:00　　　　預定在工廠會議室開會。生產部經理以及所有領班將參加。

下午6:00　　　　接著在員工餐飲部聚餐。

3月8日，星期四　　（大阪到廣島）

早上9:30　　　　李比利將去接你，送你到火車站。（日本國營鐵路）

早上10:00　　　搭新幹線離開大阪

早上12:00　　　抵達廣島。

公司經理吳約翰，將到車站會見你，載你到廣島飯店。在飯店吃晚餐。

下午2:00　　　　參觀在廣島的所有公司。

預定在會議室開會。（6號檔案有這個分公司的統計資料及進度報告）

下午6:00　　　　在廣島飯店鑽石廳，公司聚餐。

（7號檔案有演講稿。）

3月9日，星期五　　　（廣島）
　　空閒的一天
　　早上 10:00　　　　離開飯店去觀光。
　　中午 12:00　　　　在廣島鄉村俱樂部吃午餐。
　　下午 1:00　　　　與吳先生、吳太太一起打高爾夫球。
　　下午 6:00　　　　約好在吳家吃晚餐。
　　　　　　　　　　　（電話 51 ─ 0371）

3月10日，星期六　　（廣島─東京）
　　早上 10:00　　　　吳約翰將去接你，送你到火車站。（日本
　　　　　　　　　　國營鐵路）
　　早上 10:30　　　　搭新幹線離開廣島，前往東京。
　　下午 2:30　　　　抵達東京。行政部經理俞先生將到火車站
　　　　　　　　　　會見你，並載你到東京總公司。
　　下午 4:00　　　　在總公司跟全體行政人員開會。
　　　　　　　　　　（8 號檔案）
　　下午 6:00　　　　與全體行政人員在統一飯店，公司聚餐，
　　　　　　　　　　（訂好一間雙人套房）

3月11日，星期日　　（東京─台北）
　　早上 9:30　　　　總經理趙湯姆，將到飯店接你，送你到成
　　　　　　　　　　田國際機場。
　　早上 11:30　　　　到機場候機處辦理登記。
　　中午 12:30　　　　啓程。
　　　　　　　　　　115 班次國泰航空公司班機。
　　　　　　　　　　（頭等艙，供應午餐）

✦　　　　　✦　　　　　✦

【註】　luncheon〔ˈlʌntʃən〕*n.* 中餐　　conference〔ˈkɑnfərəns〕*n.* 會談
　　　　schedule〔ˈskɛdʒul〕*vt.* 安排　　statistics〔stəˈtɪstɪks〕*n.* 統計
　　　　appointment〔əˈpɔɪntmənt〕*n.* 約會

秘書必備常識

名片和頭銜是商業人士的顏面

■ **外國人的名片以工作內容為重點**

　　名片上的頭銜似乎很難處理，要怎樣清清楚楚地表明職稱，才能讓外國人明白呢？這就是在製作名片時令人傷腦筋的地方。

　　國人似乎有亂給名片的傾向，名片上總不外乎自我標榜，並以表現自己身份為重點。外國則以自己擔任的工作為名片的主要內容。由此可以看出國人的浮誇，不如外國人實際。

　　國人堅奉年資及終生奉獻為金科玉律，和外國人的實務主義完全相反。因此，在他們看來，如果定要將地位和工作內容同時列入小小的名片，似乎不太恰當。不過，學學外國人儘量以工作內容為重點，製作純西式的名片才是正確的方向。

■ **如何將職稱代換成英文**

　　首先，談談總經理的頭銜。一般來說，Manager of General Affairs 或者 Manager of Administration 都沒有錯。但是若以工作內容為重點的話，應為 Manager, Administrative Div. 或 Manager of Administration 為佳。

　　至於經理、課長、科長、主任又該如何翻譯呢？不論您被指派的工作是否配有部屬，是否擁有個人的辦公室，都可以用 manager，如：

- Manager, Overseas Division （國外部經理，海外經理）
- Manager, Canada Dept., International Division（國際部門駐加拿大經理）

其次是次長，如果是經理不在時，全權代理的人就稱 Assistant Manager。若是待遇比照次長或居輔佐經理、課長之位者，稱為 Assistant to the Manager, Chemical Division。

以下將台灣各大企業的職稱整理出來，列出一覽表：

榮譽會長 ⇨ Honorary Chairman and Director of the Company

會　　長 ⇨ Chairman and Representative Managing Director

　　　　⇨ Chairman

　　　　⇨ Chairman of the Board and Chief Executive Officer

　　　　⇨ Chairman of the Board

副 主 席 ⇨ Vice Chairman

董 事 長 ⇨ President

　　　　⇨ President and Representative Director

副董事長 ⇨ Executive Vice President

　　　　⇨ Executive Vice President and Representative Director

專任經理 ⇨ Senior Vice President

　　　　⇨ Senior Managing Director

常務經理 ⇨ Managing Director and Vice President

　　　　⇨ Managing Director

經　　理 ⇨ Director and Vice President

　　　　⇨ Director

主任秘書 ⇨ Executive Assistant to the President

秘書室（課）⇨ Secretariat（Secretary Section）

銷售（營業）部總經理 ⇨ General Sales Manager

銷售（營業）部經理 ⇨ Manager, Sales Division

產品（開發）部長 ⇨ Product Manager

總　務　部 ⇨ Administrative Div.

財　務　部 ⇨ Financial Div.

經　理　部 ⇨ Accounting Div.

人　事　部 ⇨ Recruitment Planning & Personnel Development Div.

⇨ Personnel Administration, Personnel Div.

企　劃　部 ⇨ Planning Div.

商品開發部 ⇨ Products Development Div.

企劃推展部 ⇨ Projects Development Div.

製　造　部 ⇨ Production Div.

海外事業部 ⇨ Overseas Enterprise

國　際　部 ⇨ International Div.

宣傳、廣告部 ⇨ Advertising Div.

電算機室 ⇨ Electronic Data Processing Dept.（EDP）

員工福利部 ⇨ Employees Relations Dept.

分　公　司 ⇨ Regional Sales Office, Branch Office

⑥ 上司不在時處理信件

1. 寄出對方要求的資料

【秘書須知】

- *be away from the office until July* 23
  ☞　　不在公司,到 7 月 23 日才來

- *the data you requested in his absence*
  ☞　　當他不在時,你所要的資料

- *in the meantime*　☞　　同時
- *I hope the enclosed data will be of some use to you*
  ☞　　我希望附上的資料對你有所助益

實　　例

July 5, 19 —

Dear Mr. Austin,

Since Mr. Smith is away from the office until July 23, I am sending you the data you requested in his absence. As soon as he returns, I'll ask him if there is any more information we could provide.

In the meantime, I hope the enclosed data will be of some use to you.

If there's anything further I can do to help until
Mr. Smith returns, please don't hesitate to let me
know.

                        Sincerely,

                        Lily Wu
                        Secretary to Mr. Smith

因為史密斯先生不在公司，直到 7 月 23 日才回來,因此當他不在
的時候，你所要的資料由我寄上。他一回來，我將問他**我們**是否有其
他資料可提供。

同時，我希望附上的資料，對你有所助益。

在史密斯先生回來之前，如果還要我幫忙的話，請不要猶豫，讓
我知道。

【註】 request 〔rɪˈkwɛst〕 v. 要求

hesitate 〔ˈhɛzə͵tet〕 v. 遲疑；猶豫

2. 轉交信函，徵得同意

【秘書須知】

· *be away from the office on vacation*

   ☞   不在公司，去渡假

· *pass this correspondence along to ～*

   ☞   這封信轉交給～

實 例

January 20, 19—

Dear Mr. Robertson,

   Thank you for your letter of January 17 to Mr. Wilson.

   Mr. Wilson is away from the office on vacation.

   Since he will not be back for three weeks, I am passing this correspondence along to Mr. Frank, assistant manager, who, I believe, will enjoy reading your letter and give you some information you need.

Very truly yours,

Linda Yeh
Secretary to Mr. Wilson

🖋 感謝你 1 月 17 日給威爾遜先生的來信。

　　威爾遜先生現在去渡假，不在公司。

　　因爲他三個星期後才回來，因此我把這封信轉交給副經理法蘭克先生。我相信，他會高興看到你的信，並提供你所需要的資料。

【註】　correspondence 〔,kɔrə'spɑndəns〕 *n.* 書信
　　　　assistant 〔ə'sɪstənt 〕 *adj.* 輔助的

3. 等待上司親自回覆

【秘書須知】

· ***bring it to his attention when he returns***
　☞　　當他回來時，提請他注意

實　例

April 23, 19—

Dear Mr Graham,

　　In Mr. Martin's absence, I am acknowledging receipt of your letter of April 20.

I will bring it to his attention when he returns early next week.

Very truly yours,

Nancy Lin
Secretary

馬丁先生不在時，感謝你 4 月 20 日的來信。

下星期初當他回來時，我會提請他注意。

✦　　　　✦　　　　✦

【註】　acknowledge〔ək'nɑlɪdʒ〕*v.* 致函或宣布收到；函謝

〰〰〰 學習出版，天天進步 〰〰〰

EXERCISE 5

1. 謝謝您6月6日的來信。

目前陳先生正在渡假，6月20日之前不會來上班。因為他大約兩週不來上班，我把您的信轉交給副經理江先生。

陳先生若來上班，一定會拜讀來信，並感謝您寄來的資料。

【提示】

· 目前在渡假，不會來上班

☞　**be away from the office on vacation**

· 因為他大約兩週不會來上班

☞　**since he will not be back for about two weeks**

· 我將信轉交給副經理江先生。☞　**I passed your letter along to Mr. Chiang, assistant manager.**

· 他來上班時，一定會感謝您寄來的資料。

☞　**Upon his return, I know he will appreciate your sending information to him.**

2. 已收到您8月13日的來信，但葉先生現在休假中。

下週初他回來上班，我會提請他注意。

【提示】

· 下週初他回來上班，提請他注意 ☞　**bring it to his attention when he returns early next week**

7) 預約旅館

1. 預約旅館信函

【秘書須知】

- **book a single room with bath** ☞ 　訂一間單人套房

- **the 2nd of October, inclusive** ☞ 　連10月2日在內

- **our executives** ☞ 　我們經理主管級人員

- **normally** 〔 ′nɔrməlɪ 〕 *adv.* 通常

- **by return** ☞ 　接到信之後；立刻

實 例

The Manager,
Mayflower Hotel,
Thames Road,
Broadworth,
Goss-shine,
England JE5 OAJ

23rd August, 19 —

Dear Sir,

　I would like to book a single room with bath from the 28th of September to the 2nd of October, inclusive, for Mr. Martin White, our Export Manager.

As you know, our executives normally stay at the Mayflower Hotel when in London.

We would like you to provide a room on the first floor, overlooking Hyde Park, if possible.

As he will have many business meetings, he would like you to reserve a room for conference for the period of his stay.

Mr. White will arrive in the evening of the 28th September and is intending to leave in the late afternoon on the 3rd October.

You may remember that he stayed at your hotel last year.

We should be greatly obliged if you would let us have your current prices including service charges.

I would like you to confirm this booking by return.

Yours truly,

Rebecca Lin
Secretary to Mr. White

我想替本公司外銷部經理馬丁‧懷特先生，訂一間單人套房，從9月28日到10月2日為止（連10月2日在內）。

如你所知，我們的經理主管級人員在倫敦，通常住在五月花旅館。

如果可能的話，本公司希望你們提供一間在一樓，可以俯瞰海德公園的房間。

因為他將有許多商業會議，所以他希望在停留期間內，你們能保留一個房間，作為開會之用。

懷特先生將在9月28日傍晚抵達，並且要在10月3日午後離開。

你們可能記得，去年他曾住在你們旅館。

如果你們能讓本公司獲悉目前貴旅館包括服務費在內的價格，我們將不勝感激。

我希望貴旅館接到信之後，請即確認此一預約。

◆　　　◆　　　◆

【註】 inclusive〔ɪnˈklusɪv〕*adj.* 包括的
overlook〔͵ovɚˈlʊk〕*v.* 俯視；俯瞰

2. 旅館的回覆函

【秘書須知】

· *accommodate* 〔 ə'kɑmə,det 〕 *v.* 留宿

· *we have pleasure in confirming* ～ ☞　　我們樂於確認～

· *confirm the reservation of* ☞　　確認預約

· *This price covers breakfast.* ☞　　這個價錢包含早餐。

· *will be available daily* ☞　　白天可資使用

實　例

Miss Rebecca Lin

The International Chemical Co., Ltd.

Bright Building,

220 Tun Hwa South Road,

Taipei, Taiwan, R.O.C.

30th August ,19 —

Dear Miss Lin,

　　Thank you for your letter of the 23rd August.

　　We were very glad to hear from you again, and to

know that Mr. White wishes to accommodate once

again at our hotel.

We have pleasure in confirming the reservation of a single room on the first floor, overlooking Hyde Park as requested, which I am sure Mr. White will find completely satisfactory.

The cost of a single room with bath is £20 per night including a service charge of 15 percent. This price covers breakfast.

A conference room will be available daily.

We look forward to seeing Mr. White.

Yours faithfully,

Thomas Green
Manager

Enclosures: Tariff card
Illustrated brochure

謝謝妳 8 月 23 日來信。

我們很高興再度收到妳的來信,並且知道懷特先生希望再住在我們旅館。

　　　　我們樂於確認，妳預約一間在一樓的單人房，如妳所要求的，可

以俯瞰海德公園。我有把握，懷特先生將會發現完全令人滿意。

　　　　單人套房一間價格是每晚 20 英磅，連百分之十五的服務費在內。

這個價格包括早餐。

　　　　有一間會議室，白天可資使用。

　　　　我們期待見到懷特先生。

附上：關稅卡

　　　　圖解小冊子

【註】　satisfactory〔ˌsætɪsˈfæktərɪ〕*adj.* 令人滿意的

　　　　reservation〔ˌrɛzəˈveʃən〕*n.* 預約

　　　　brochure〔broˈʃʊr〕*n.*〔法文〕小冊子（=*pamphlet*）（ = *pamphlet*）

---

3. 預約舉辦會議的地點

【秘書須知】

- *executive suite* ☞ 　最高級套房

- *make arrangements for* ☞ 　安排

- *U-shaped table* ☞ 　馬蹄型的桌子

實　例

March 10, 19 —

Reservations Manager
The Palace Hotel
43 Fadem Road Springfield,
New Jersey 06051
U.S.A.

Reservations for a Conference Room

Gentlemen,

Please reserve your largest executive suite for
June 19 and 20, 19 —.

After seeing your excellent facilities the other
day, our executive manager, Mr. James Smith has
recommended your hotel as the conference site of this
year for all the managers of the branch.

Would you please make arrangements for a conference room with a " U-shaped table " for 20 persons?

An early confirmation of this reservation would be
much appreciated.

Yours sincerely,

Nancy Chen

預 約 會 議 室

請在 19 — , 6 月 19、20 兩天,預留一間最大最高級的套房。

我們行政經理詹姆士・史密斯先生,幾天前在看過你們完善的設施之後,推薦貴旅館作為今年所有分公司經理會議的地點。

請你們安排一間有一張可以坐 20 個人的馬蹄型桌子的會議室。

若你們能儘早確認此一預約,則感幸甚。

◆   ◆   ◆

【註】 facility〔fəˈsɪlətɪ〕*n*.(*pl*.)設施   ***the other day*** 幾天前
recommend〔ˌrɛkəˈmɛnd〕*v*. 推薦   site〔saɪt〕*n*. 地點
appreciate〔əˈpriʃɪˌet〕*v*. 感激

EXERCISE 6

1.　　本公司董事長及副董事長9月要到紐約，參觀世界貿易商展，請您預備兩間附有浴室的房間，如果可能的話，也請在同一層樓安排一間秘書的單人房。

　　可否預約9月10日到9月15日的房間，請速告知，希望也在回信中告知詳細的費用。

【提示】

- 到紐約參觀世界貿易商展
  ☞　　*will be visiting New York for the World Trade Fair*

- 可能的話在同一層樓
  ☞　　*on the same floor if possible*

- 可否預約9月10日到9月15日的房間
  ☞　　*whether you can reserve this accommodation from 10 to 15 September inclusive*

- 樂於在回信中得知詳細的費用
  ☞　　*be glad to have a reply with details on charges*

2.　　陳先生於5月3日因商務訪羅馬，這次也希望投宿貴飯店。如果能讓他住去年那個房間最好，否則後面的任何一間也可以，因為前面的房間面對大街，稍嫌吵雜。

　　請速回覆，以便完成陳先生的旅行安排。

【提示】

- 希望能投宿貴飯店
  - ☞ hope that you will be able to accommodate him

- 如果能讓他住去年那間房間
  - ☞ if you can let him have the same room as last year

- 否則就是後面的任何一間
  - ☞ or in any case a room at the back of the hotel

- 因為前面的房間面對大街，稍嫌吵雜
  - ☞ as the front rooms on the main street are rather noisy

- 以便完成陳先生的旅行安排
  - ☞ so that I can complete arrangements for Mr. Chen's visit

3. 眞高興又聽到您的訊息，並且您要再一次光臨本飯店。

很抱歉，去年住的那間房間已在您指定的日期被預約了，但是同一層還有一間大的單人套房，我相信您一定會非常滿意，事實上，這間比去年住的房間更安靜，因此，我為您保留了這一間。

期待 5 月 3 日見到您。

【提示】

- 眞高興又聽到您的消息
  - ☞ I was glad to hear from you again

- 您要再一次光臨本飯店
  ☞ *you wish to be accommodated once more at our hotel*

- 您談到的日期
  ☞ *the nights in question*

- 我相信您一定會非常滿意
  ☞ *I am sure you will find completely satisfactory*

- 爲您保留了這一間
  ☞ *hold this room for you*

- 期待見到您
  ☞ *expect to see you*

4.　本公司銷售經理陳俊田先生，將因商務停留丹佛十天。請求預約從 10 月 30 日到 11 月 9 日，套房一間，希望儘早確認此一預約。

【提示】

- 因商務停留丹佛十天
  ☞ *will be in Denver on business for len days*

- 希望儘早確認此一預約
  ☞ *be glad if you could confirm this booking as soon as possible*

秘書必備常識

秘書不穿制服，應著自己搭配的服飾

▨ 請問外國客人喜歡喝什麼咖啡

從前只要一提到秘書就聯想到茶和咖啡，最近則似乎將這份工作委任小弟、小妹來做，主要是由於辦公室分工細密的結果。但是，爲了讓會長、董事長、經理、副理等階級的主管更舒適，給來訪的賓客更好的印象，這份工作仍然應該屬於秘書。

如果遇有外國客戶，秘書也要親自調配咖啡，服飾上也需特別注意，最好不要穿制服，選擇自己搭配的服飾方爲上策，因爲外國人看到穿制服的人，難免以爲是公司中地位較低的職員或小妹，應特別注意。

▨ 將冲調咖啡格式化

外國人對咖啡的調配各有喜好，所以應該詢問：How would you like your coffee made?或 Shall we make it black or regular？（black 是不加糖和奶精的咖啡，而 regular 則是加糖和奶精的咖啡）

歐美的秘書經常對公司生產力的提昇多所貢獻，能力很强，但對於上司的服務也極其盡心，甚至於上司對咖啡的偏好及調理也格式化（ in written form），寫得清清楚楚，以防自己若卸任的話，新任秘書也能調配出令上司滿意的咖啡。這種敬業精神值得國內秘書多方學習。

8) 預約飛機座位

1. 爲上司預約前往紐約的飛機

【秘書須知】

- *sales representative* ☞　業務代表；銷售代表

- *on the earliest flight possible* ☞　搭乘愈早的班機

- *submit your account directly to them*
  ☞　你把帳單直接交給他們

＊＊＊＊＊＊＊＊＊＊＊＊＊ 實　例 ＊＊＊＊＊＊＊＊＊＊＊＊＊

The Reservations Manager,

Atokins Travel,

70 Bond Street,

London, W1, 8HT.

July 15th, 19—

Dear Sir,

　　Two of our sales representatives, Mr. Mark Liu and Mr. Ned Lee would like to fly from London to New York on the earliest flight possible.

We would be obliged if you would book two economy class seats for them on a flight leaving London on or about July 28th.

The International Bank, London, has been instructed to pay the fare and booking fee, and we would ask you to submit your account directly to them.

We appreciate your early confirmation.

Yours truly,

Ruth Lin

Secretary

本公司的兩位業務代表,劉馬克和李奈德先生,希望搭乘愈早的班機,從倫敦飛往紐約。

如果你能爲他們預訂兩個經濟客艙的座位,在 7 月 28 日當天或者前後幾天,飛離倫敦的話,則感幸甚。

我們已叫倫敦國際銀行,付費用和預約款項,請你把帳單直接交給他們。

我們感激你早日確認。

【註】 economy class 經濟客艙

confirmation〔͵kɑnfəˈmeʃən〕*n.* 確定;認可

2. 預約的旅行社回覆

【秘書須知】

* *we have for acknowledgment your letter dated ~*

  ☞　　我們已收到你～月～日的來函

  ⇨ acknowledged your order No. 100　收到你第100號的訂單

  ⇨ acknowledged（receipt of）your check for $400

  　　收到你美金400元的支票

* *The account will be sent to ~*　☞　　帳單將送到～

✕✕✕✕✕✕✕✕✕✕✕✕✕✕ **實　例** ✕✕✕✕✕✕✕✕✕✕✕✕✕✕

20th July, 19 —

Dear Miss Lin,

　　We have for acknowledgment your letter dated July 15th requesting us to book economy-class seats for Mr. Mark Liu and Mr. Ned Lee on a flight from London to New York.

　　Two seats have been reserved on flight B.A. 917 departing Heathrow Airport, London at 10:00 a.m. on the 28th, arriving New York at 11:00 a.m. local time on the 29th.

The account will be sent to the International Bank, London, as requested.

Yours faithfully,

Josef Watson

Reservations Manager

我們已收到妳 7 月 15 日的來函，要求我們為劉馬克先生和李奈德先生，訂經濟客艙的座位，從倫敦飛往紐約。

已保留英航 917 次班機的兩個座位，該班機於 28 日早上 10 點從倫敦希斯洛機場起飛，於 29 日當地時間早上 11 點，抵達紐約。

如妳所要求的，帳單將送到倫敦國際銀行。

◆　　　◆　　　◆

【註】　B.A. = *British Airlines* 英國航空公司

　　　depart 〔 dɪ'pɑrt 〕 *v.* 離開；啓程

　　　local 〔 'lokḷ 〕 *adj.* 地方的；當地的

3. 請求變更預約

【秘書須知】

- *arrange a seat on the same flight*
  ☞   安排同一班次飛機的一個座位

- *make the necessary alteration* ☞   做必須的變動

✗✗✗✗✗✗✗✗✗✗✗✗✗ **實   例** ✗✗✗✗✗✗✗✗✗✗✗✗✗

August 29, 19—

Gentlemen,

Just a month ago, I booked a flight to Melbourne

by NWA on 704 for Saturday 4th September for Mr.

Chao, our Overseas Manager.

He has now decided to stay longer in Hawaii and

would like to fly by the same flight two weeks later.

I should be very much obliged if you would arrange

a seat on the same flight for the 18th September.

I enclose his ticket and would be grateful if you could make the necessary alteration.

Yours truly,

Linda Lee
Secretary to Mr. Chao

正好在一個月以前，我爲本公司海外部經理趙先生，訂了9月4日星期六，西北航空公司704班次飛機，飛往墨爾本。

他現已決定在夏威夷多停留一段時間，並希望能在兩星期後，搭乘同一班次飛機。

如果你能安排9月18日同一班次飛機的一個座位，我將不勝感激。

附上他的機票，如能做必須的變動，則不勝感激。

✦　　　✦　　　✦

【註】Melbourne 〔 'mɛlbən 〕 n. 墨爾本 (澳洲東南部一港都)
NWA= *Northwest Airlines* 西北航空公司
alteration 〔 ˌɔltəˈreʃən 〕 n. 改變

4. 變更預約的回函

【秘書須知】

- *is fully booked* ☞　　客滿；全部訂完
- *suggest alternatives where there are seats available*
  ☞　　建議其他尚有座位可資利用的選擇

✕✕✕✕✕✕✕✕✕✕✕✕✕✕ 實　例 ✕✕✕✕✕✕✕✕✕✕✕✕✕✕

September 5, 19 ─

Dear Miss Lee,

　　We regret to inform you that the flight you requested is fully booked, and there are at present no cancellations.

　　We would like to suggest alternatives where there are seats available.

　　Pan American Airways Flight No. PA 560 has seats available on the same day departing Honolulu at 19:45.

I look forward to hearing from you as soon as possible.

Yours truly,

John Smith

Reservations Manager

我們很抱歉通知妳，妳所要求的班次，座位已全部訂完，而目前無人取消預約。

我們想建議其他尚有座位可資利用的選擇。

泛美航空公司在同一天 19：45，從檀香山起飛的 560 次班機，尚有座位。

我希望能儘快接到妳的信。

◆   ◆   ◆

【註】　cancellation〔͵kænsə'leʃən〕*n*. 作廢；取消

alternative〔æl'tɜ˞nətɪv〕*n*.（*pl*.）選擇

EXERCISE 7

1.　　本公司出口部經理陳茂和先生，擬於 3 月 4 日由洛杉磯，搭乘貴公司於當天上午 10 點 30 分飛往芝加哥的 523 次班機，並搭 3 月 8 日下午 3 點 45 分起飛的 716 次班機，由芝加哥返回洛杉磯。煩請預定一個頭等艙位。

　　機票費請向本公司洛杉磯分公司索取。

　　麻煩您確定這件事。

【提示】

・預定一個頭等艙位

　☞　　*reserve first-class space*（ *seat* ）

・由芝加哥返回洛杉磯

　☞　　*return from Chicago to Los Angeles*

・機票費向～索取

　☞　　*the ticket should be charged to ~*

・確認此一預約

　☞　　*confirm this reservation*

2.　　本公司研究開發部經理林三和先生，下週到達巴黎，而後前往倫敦。因此，煩請預定一個 21 日左右由巴黎往倫敦的班機座位。

　　費用與預定款項，我方已指示巴黎國際銀行代爲支付給貴方。

先爲您處理此事致上謝意。

【提示】

- 然後前往倫敦
  ☞ *will then go on to London*

- 因此 ☞ *therefore*

- 費用與預約款項的帳單
  ☞ *your account for the fare and booking fee*

- 指示巴黎國際銀行代爲支付給貴方
  ☞ *will be paid by the International Bank, Paris, who have instructions to do so on our behalf*

- 先爲您關照此事致上謝意。
  ☞ *We thank you in advance for your attention to this matter.*

秘書必備常識

數字的讀法與寫法

▓ 　小數目的讀法

　　雖然我國現行學校教育對數字並未特別強調，但是，在實際生活中若忽視數字，經常會壞事。對交易而言更是差之毫釐，失之千里。特於此處詳細說明數字的讀法與寫法。

▓ 　基數（Cardinal Numbers）

1	one	16	sixteen
2	two	17	seventeen
3	three	18	eighteen
4	four	19	nineteen
5	five	20	twenty
6	six	21	twenty-one
7	seven	22	twenty-two
8	eight	23	twenty-three
9	nine	24	twenty-four
10	ten	25	twenty-five
11	eleven	26	twenty-six
12	twelve	27	twenty-seven
13	thirteen	28	twenty-eight
14	fourteen	29	twenty-nine
15	fifteen	30	thirty

31	thirty-one etc.	80	eighty
40	forty	90	ninety
50	fifty	100	a hundred
60	sixty	1,000	a thousand
70	seventy	1,000,000	a million

組合以上數字：

600 ······ six hundred

135 ······ one hundred and thirty-five

170 ······ one hundred and seventy

204 ······ two hundred and four

1,008 ······ one thousand and eight

1,081 ······ one thousand and eighty-one

4,000 ······ four thousand

50,135 ······ fifty thousand, one hundred and thirty-five

　　讀者必須特別注意，只有單一的 hundred, thousand 的時候，通常前面要加 *a* 而非 one，若加入其他數字時，要用 **one**。

　　還有一點需特別小心，讀寫三位以上的數字時，hundred 之後要加 and。若無 hundred 位，則 thousand 之後要接 and。

▓ **數字很大的讀法**

　　通常 hundred, thousand, million 是不用複數的。但遇到籠統的大數目時，可用複數並加上 of，譬如「幾百人」是 hundreds of people，「幾千封信」是 thousands of letters。若為確切數字，則 hundred 或 thousand 之後不必加 of。

　10,000 ······ ten thousand

　100,000 ······ one hundred thousand

　150,000 ······ one hundred and fifty thousand

　1,000,000 ······ one million

　10,000,000 ······ ten million

657,876,342 ······ six hundred and fifty-seven million, eight hundred and seventy-six thousand, three hundred and forty-two

　　在美國，billion 代表億，在英國則代表兆。trillion 在美國是兆，在英國是百萬兆。

　　3 位以上的序數和基數一樣，要用 and。例如，第 101 號（101 st）是 the hundred and first。

■　**小數點的讀法**

　　小數點讀成 point。以下各數字要分別唸出。

　　1.14 ······ one point one four

　　0.092 ······ nought（zero, 0）point nought nine two

■　**數字加單位的讀法**

　　日常生活中最常用到的是金錢和溫度單位。

　　26°C ······ twenty-six degrees Centigrade

　　18°F ······ eighteen degrees Fahrenheit

　　-8° ······ eight degrees below zero

　　p. 91 l. 4（91 頁第 4 行）······ page ninety-one line four

$6.72 …… six dollars and seventy two cents

£3 5s · 4p……three pounds five shillings four pence

■ 序數（ Ordinal Numbers ）的讀法

最後複習一部分序數。

✗ first (1st), second (2nd), third (3rd)

✗ fourth (4th), fifth (5th), seventh (7th)

✗ eighth (8th), ninth (9th), tenth (10th)

✗ eleventh (11th), twelfth (12th),

✗ thirteenth (13th)…… twentieth (20th)

✗ twenty-first (21st)

9) 紀念酒會邀請與回覆

1. 最正式的邀請函

【秘書須知】

- *R.S.V.P.* ☞　法文之 Répondez, s'il vous plaît
  (*please reply*) 的略語，其意爲「敬請回覆」。亦可寫成 *Enclosed reply* 或 *enclosed card*,「附上答覆卡」的意思。若是
  想要求被邀請者回覆給秘書，可寫成 R.S.V.P Secretary to ～
  (如實例1)，或是 R.S.V.P to the Secretary of ～, 若是回
  覆給董事長室，則寫 R.S.V.P. President's Office。向被邀請
  者特別表示，希望幾點以前列席時，要在 R.S.V.P 之外，加註
  Guests should be seated by 5:20 p.m. (來賓應在午後5:20
  以前入席)。

實例(1)

Mr. John Liu

Chairman of the Board of Chu Kang Glass Company Limited

requests the pleasure of the company of

Mr. Howard Thomas

on the occasion of the inauguration of

Chu Kang Glass Company at the Palace Hotel

```
                          *
            on Wednesday, March 2, 19 —

              18:30—19:30 Cocktails

                  19:45 Dinner

  R.S.V.P.

  Secretary to John Liu            Black Tie
```

巨剛玻璃有限公司，劉約翰先生，敬邀豪爾德‧湯瑪斯先生的公司同仁光臨，巨剛玻璃公司於豪華飯店舉行的開幕典禮。

```
                          *
              19 — , 3 月 2 日，星期三
              18:30 — 19:30  雞尾酒
                  19:45  晚宴
```

【註】 在此種邀請函上，需一一填寫被邀請者的姓名，若要加註「希望～蒞臨指
　　　教」，則要在＊處加上 in the presence of ～。
　　　inauguration〔ɪnˌɔgjəˈreʃən〕*n.* 開幕典禮；就職典禮
　　　cocktail〔ˈkɑkˌtel〕*n.* 雞尾酒
　　　black tie 黑領帶；(男人的)配著黑領帶的一種半正式禮服

【秘書須知】

- *To commemorate the Eightieth Anniversary*
  ☞　慶祝80週年紀念

- *request the pleasure of your company at* ～
  ☞　敬邀貴公司同仁光臨 ～

實例(2)

To Commemorate the Eightieth Anniversary

Mr. Gavin Lin, President

of

Pei Shao Motor Co., Ltd.

requests the pleasure of your company

at a cocktail party

on Saturday, April 10

at 5:30 to 7:30 p.m.

at the Palace Hotel

to express thanks and appreciation

R.S.V.P.　　　　　　Please present this card

Enclosed reply card　　at the entrance to Orchid

　　　　　　　　　　Room in the Hotel

🖮　　爲慶祝 80 週年紀念，北劭電機有限公司董事長，林蓋文先生，敬
邀貴公司同仁光臨，於 4 月 10 日，星期六午後 5:30 到 7:30 在豪華飯
店舉行的雞尾酒會，以表謝意和感激。

敬請回覆　　　　　　　　　　　　請將此卡交到該飯店
附答覆卡　　　　　　　　　　　　蘭花廳的入口處

◆　　　　◆　　　　◆

【註】　若非邀請特定的人參加，而是邀請多數的同仁參加，則不必一一填寫姓名，
以填寫 request the pleasure of your company 爲佳。
entrance〔'ɛntrəns〕 *n.* 入口；大門

2. 出席者正式回函

【秘書須知】

・ *accept with pleasure* 🖝　　樂於接受

實　例

Mr. *James Stone* *
accepts with pleasure
Mr. Rufus Johnson's
kind invitation to
a cocktail party
on Saturday, April 10
at 5:30 to 7:30 p.m.
at the Palace Hotel

詹姆斯・史東先生樂於接受魯法斯・江遜先生親切的邀請，參加於 4 月 10 日，星期六，下午 5:30 到 7:30 在豪華飯店舉辦的雞尾酒會。

✦　　✦　　✦

【註】 ＊部分需用親筆簽名

invitation〔͵ɪnvə'teʃən〕 *n*. 邀請

3. 缺席者正式回函

【秘書須知】

・ *be unable to* ☞ 　　不能的；無法於

實　例

Mr. *James Stone*

regrets that he is unable to accept

Mr. Rufus Johnson's

kind invitation to

a cocktail party

on Saturday, April 10

at 5:30 to 7:30 p.m.

at the Palace Hotel

🖅　詹姆斯・史東先生，對無法接受魯法斯・江遜先生的邀請，參加於 4 月 10 日，星期六，下午 5:30 到 7:30 於豪華酒店舉辦的雞尾酒會，表示遺憾。

◆　　　　◆　　　　◆

【註】　regret〔rɪˈgrɛt〕*v.* 悔恨；惋惜；抱歉

4. 附有祝賀詞的出席回函

【秘書須知】

- *the directors and officers* ☞　董事們和人員

- *extend their warmest congratulations on~*
  ☞　在～表示（申明）最衷心的恭賀之意（正式社交信件中，不用 *our*，而用第三人稱 *their*）

- *(extend) their very best wishes for success and prosperity* ☞　（表示）祝福成功、興盛

- *function*〔ˈfʌŋkʃən〕*n.*（*pl.*）儀式；慶典；宴會

實 例

April 10, 19—

Gentlemen,

　　The directors and officers of Tun Chui Chemical Co. Ltd., are happy to extend their warmest congratulations on the occasion of the Golden Jubilee of your organization

[圖] 4. 模範秘書英語書信 *153*

and their very best wishes for success and prosperity in the years to come.

Representing Tun Chui Chemical Co., Ltd., Mr. Neil Chiang , Manager of San Francisco Branch, is delighted to attend the functions to be held at the Hotel Sheraton.

We sincerely hope our pleasant business relationship will continue for many years to come.

With kind regards,

Neil Chiang

Manager

San Francisco Branch

在貴機構五十週年紀念大典之際，敦佳化學有限公司的董事們和人員，樂於表示最衷心的恭賀之意，並且祝福未來成功、興隆。

舊金山分公司經理江尼爾先生，很高興能代表敦佳化學有限公司，參加於喜來登飯店舉行的宴會。。

我們誠摯希望，我們之間愉快的業務往來關係，在未來將持續不輟。

✦　　✦　　✦

【註】 prosperity〔prɑsˊperətɪ〕*n.* 繁榮；興盛；順遂

the Golden Jubilee 五十週年紀念大典

5. 來往銀行的祝賀函

【秘書須知】

- *silver anniversary* ☞　二十五週年紀念
- *It's common knowledge that ~*
  =*It's a matter of common knowledge that ~*
  ☞　大家都知道

實　例

May 15, 19—

Gentleman,

It's a pleasure to send you our sincere congratulations on the silver anniversary of Sunlight Trading Company.

We at the International Bank consider it our good fortune to have had you as a customer for the last ten of those twenty-five years.

It's common knowledge that Sunlight Trading Company is one of the most respected firms in the country.

Your company has made steady progress and growth.

We look forward to a pleasant relationship for another 25 years to come.

Cordially,

．．．．．．．．．．．．．．．．．．．

在陽光貿易公司廿五週年紀念之際，很高興獻上我們誠摯的祝福。

我們國際銀行的同仁認爲，在那廿五年的後十年，有您這位顧客，是我們的幸運。

大家都知道陽光貿易公司，是全國最受敬重的公司之一。

貴公司一直穩健地進步和成長。

我們期待未來另一個廿五年關係愉快。

✦　　　✦　　　✦

【註】　customer〔ˈkʌstəmɚ〕 *n.* 顧客
　　　　steady〔ˈstɛdɪ〕 *adj.* 穩健的；股實的

EXERCISE 8

1.　　國際貿易股份有限公司董事長暨全體員工，為紀念創立150周年，於19一年5月5日，星期四下午7點半，假三普飯店舉行招待會，煩請各位列席參加，並予通知。

　　　服裝不必拘泥。

請寄董事會秘書

【提示】

- 紀念國際貿易股份有限公司創立 150 周年
    ☞ *mark the **150th** anniversary of the founding of the International Trading Company Limited*

- 董事會秘書
    ☞ *The secretary to the Board*

2.　　在貴公司創立90周年令人歡欣之際，獻上我衷心的祝福。

【提示】

- 在貴公司創立90周年令人歡欣之際
    ☞ *on the happy occasion of the Company's **90th** anniversary*

- 獻上我衷心的祝福
    ☞ *write to convey to you my heartiest congratulations*

3.　　本公司創立90周年之際，收到您9月6日寄出的誠摯賀函，非常感謝。

【提示】

- 本公司創立90周年之際
  ☞　on the *90th Anniversary of the founding of our Company*

- 您於9月6日寄出的誠摯賀函
  ☞　*your kind letter of 6th September expressing your congratulations*

4.　　非常感謝陽光貿易股份有限公司董事長，邀請我參加11月6日在希爾頓飯店舉行的晚宴，我將樂於出席。

【提示】

- 樂於出席　☞　*have much pleasure in accepting*
  　　　　　☞　*be delighted to attend*

5.　　大衛·布朗夫婦非常抱歉，由於已有約定，不能參加5月7日下午8點的招待會。

【提示】

- 大衛·布朗夫婦非常抱歉～
  ☞　*Mr. and Mrs. David Brown very much regret ～*

10) 公司合併與遷移通知

1. 公司合併的通知

【秘書須知】

- *be pleased to inform you* ～ = *have pleasure in informing of the merger of A Company with B Company*

  ☞ 很高興通知你A公司與B公司合併

- *have merged with* ～ ☞ 與～合併

- *come into effect on* ～ = *go into effect on* ～

  ☞ 自～起生效

- *work upon the same line* = *do the same line of business*

  ☞ 做同一種的生意

- *there will be no change in this respect*

  ☞ 這方面不會有所更動

********************* **實 例** *********************

November 10, 19—

Gentleman,

We are pleased to inform you that Ta Yang Trading Company has merged with Hwa Wei Trading Company under the new firm name of Hwa Yang Trading Company which will come into effect on April 4th, 19—.

The two companies have been working upon the same line for many years, and there will be no change in this respect.

Very truly yours,

....

我們很高興通知你，大洋貿易公司與華偉貿易公司已合併，新公司名爲華洋貿易公司，自19—4月4日起生效。

多年來，這兩家公司一直做同一種生意，在這方面將不會有所改變。

【註】　firm〔fɜm〕*n.* 公司
line〔lain〕*n.* 生意；職業；貨
respect〔rɪ'spɛkt〕*n.* 方面

2. 公司遷移的通知

【秘書須知】

- *Sales Division* ☞　　銷售部、營業部

- *shall be in operation* ☞　　開始營業

- *we shall be pleased to receive our friends*
☞　　我們樂意接待朋友

- *remain unchanged* ☞　　保留不變

- *the management* ☞　　全體經理人員，經理一同

****************** 實例（1） *****************

3rd May, 19—

Dear Sirs,

We are pleased to announce that our Sales Division will move to King Building, Room Number 209 at 52 Sung Chiang Road, Taipei, where we shall be in operation from the 5th of May, 19—, and where we shall be pleased to receive our friends.

Our cable address remains unchanged and mail should continue to be addressed to the Post Office Box No. 52, Taipei.

The management takes this opportunity to solicit your continued support and cooperation.

Yours faithfully,

....

President

我們很高興宣佈，本銷售部將遷往台北市松江路52號帝王大廈209室，自19－5月5日開始營業，我們樂意在那裏接待朋友。

我們的海外電報簡號保留不變，郵件地址仍寫台北郵政 52 號信箱 。

全體經理人員藉此機會，懇求你繼續支持與合作 。

【註】　operation〔͵ɑpəˈreʃən〕*n*. 工作
　　　　cable address　海外電報簡號
　　　　remain〔rɪˈmen〕*v*. 保留
　　　　solicit〔səˈlɪsɪt〕*v*. 懇求

【秘書須知】

· *our Chicago Representative Office*

☞　　我們在芝加哥的代表辦事處

· *move to the following new location*

☞　　遷移到下列新地點

＊＊＊＊＊＊＊＊＊＊＊＊＊＊＊＊＊＊ 實例（2） ＊＊＊＊＊＊＊＊＊＊＊＊＊＊＊＊＊＊

March 1, 19—

The International Chemical Co., Ltd.

　We wish to inform you that from October 1, 19—, our Chicago Representative Office will move to the following new location.

Room 795, Sky Building

```
*****************************************
*                                       *
*        421 Michigan Avenue  Chicago   *
*                                       *
*     Telephone Number  Chicago 386-5697*
*                                       *
*        Telex Number  66975428 IQP     *
*                                       *
*        Cable Address  Unchanged       *
*                                       *
*****************************************
```

國際化學有限公司

📠　　我們希望通知你，自 19 — ，10 月 1 日起，我們在芝加哥的代表辦事處，將遷移到下列新地點。

　　　　芝加哥密西根大道 421 號，藍天大廈 795 室

　　　　電話號碼芝加哥 386-5697

　　　　商務交換電報號碼 66975428 IQP

　　　　海外電報簡號無變動

◆　　　　◆　　　　◆

【註】　avenue〔'ævə,nju〕n. 大道

　　　　telex〔'tɛlɪks〕n. 商務交換電報；電傳

EXERCISE 9

1.

遷 址 通 知

國際貿易股份有限公司化學藥品部將於 5 月 20 日，遷移至下列新址。

台北市忠孝東路四段 32 號 4 樓 A 15 室

電傳及電報代號不變。

2.　特為通知，本公司國外部將由總公司遷往城中區博愛路 33 號的三德貿易通商大樓，19 —年 10 月 10 日起於該大樓處營業，歡迎各位蒞臨指教。電報代號不變，郵件也請繼續投遞，台北郵政 11572 號信箱。

【提示】

・ 由總公司遷往～

　☞　*will move from our Head Office to ～*

3.　本公司很高興通知貴方，將於 3 月 1 日和台中的青山貿易股份有限公司合併，更名為國際貿易股份有限公司。

新址在台北市敦化北路 55 號。

藉此機會，全體主管人員敬祈各位一本以往，繼續給予支持與協助。

【提示】

- 很高興通知貴方～
  ☞ *have the pleasure in informing you of ～*

- 本公司與～合併
  ☞ *the merger of our company with ～*

- 新公司定名為～，新址在～。
  ☞ *The new company will be known as ～ with head-quarters at ～.*

- 藉此機會，全體經理人員敬祈各位一本以往，繼續給予支持和合作。
  ☞ *The Management takes this opportunity to solicit your continued support and cooperation.*

4. 專此通知，下列兩公司合併為陽光電子股份有限公司。

【提示】

- 下列兩公司
  ☞ *the following two companies*

- 合併為～
  ☞ *be amalgamated ～*

11) 開設分公司通知

1. 開設分公司的通知函

【秘書須知】

· **20 *years of experience in the trade***

☞　在這一行有20年的經驗

· **be *available to you from the outset***

☞　一開始即可為你服務

· ***offer you unparalleled service*** ☞　提供你空前的服務

◇◇◇◇◇◇◇◇◇◇◇◇◇ **實 例** ◇◇◇◇◇◇◇◇◇◇◇◇◇◇

March 10, 19—

Gentlemen,

On the first of next month, we are opening a new branch in your district, at 20 Chung Hsiao West Road, Taipei, just opposite the Taipei Station.

The Manager will be Mr. Joe Cannon, whose 20 years of experience in the trade will be available to you from the outset.

Our showroom will be one of the best equipped in Taipei, and we feel sure that we shall be able to offer you unparalleled service.

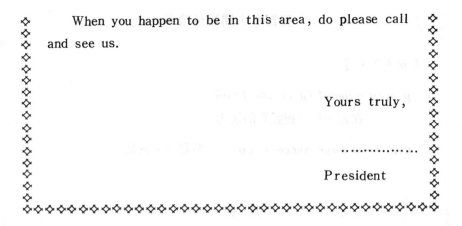

When you happen to be in this area, do please call and see us.

Yours truly,

....

President

下個月1號，我們在貴區新的分公司將開幕，地址是台北市忠孝西路20號，台北火車站正對面。

喬・坎農先生將擔任經理，他在這一行有20年的經驗，一開始即可爲你服務。

我們的貨品陳列室，將是全台北市設備最好的一個，而且我們確定，將可提供你空前的服務。

當你剛好在這個地區，請一定來拜訪、參觀。

✦　　　✦　　　✦

【註】　opposite〔'ɑpəzɪt〕*adj.* 對面的
　　　　equip〔ɪ'kwɪp〕*v.* 設備
　　　　showroom〔'ʃo,rum〕*n.* 貨品陳列室

2. 祝賀友人開設分公司

【秘書須知】

· ***proved capability in the trade***
  ☞　在這一行已經證實的能力

· ***will be a huge success*** ☞　　將是一大成功

◇◇◇◇◇◇◇◇◇◇◇◇◇◇◇◇ 實 例 ◇◇◇◇◇◇◇◇◇◇◇◇◇◇◇◇

Dear Jack,

　　How wonderful it is to learn your new branch will be open and be ready for business — congratulations !

　　With your experience and proved capability in the trade, I know your organization will be a huge success.

　　Please accept my warmest congratulations and best wishes.

　　　　　　　　　　　　　　　　　　　Sincerely,

　　　　　　　　　　　　　　　　　…………………

　　　　　　　　　　　　　　　　　President

得知你的分公司將開幕，並已準備營業，眞是太好了 — 恭喜，恭喜！

以你的經驗和在這一行已經證實的能力，我知道你的組織將是一大成功。

請接受我最衷心的恭賀和祝福。

✦　　　✦　　　✦

【註】　branch〔bræntʃ〕*n.* 分公司

　　　　huge〔hjudʒ〕*adj.* 巨大的

EXERCISE 10

1. 特此通知，本公司今天於台北設立分公司。

5月10日　國際貿易公司

【提示】

- 今天 ☞ *this day, today*

2. 本人今辭去太平洋化學股份有限公司之職，於台中開設新公司，以陽光化學公司命名，開始營業。

【提示】

- 以～命名 ☞ *under the name of ～*
- 開始營業 ☞ *start*（commence）*business*
- 辭職 ☞ *resign*（屆齡退休是 retire）

3. 剛收到您於台中體育用品店開幕的通知，恭喜！我知道這是您多年來的心願。我相信以您的商業技巧與工作熱誠，必能在短期內獲致前所未有，日趨繁榮的事業。

敬祝順利成功。

【提示】

- 體育用品店的開幕

  ☞ *the opening of your own sporting goods store*

- 多年來的心願

  ☞ *it has been a dream of yours for many years*

- 以您的商業技巧和工作熱誠

  ☞ *with your know-how and willingness to work*

- 獲致前所未有，日趨繁榮的事業

  ☞ *have a booming business which shows no sign of peaking*

- 敬祝順利成功 ☞ *good luck*

4. 若有適當的地點，本公司考慮在紐約設立分公司銷售本公司的新文字處理機。爲了實現這個計畫，若您能夠提供任何資料，則感幸甚。

【提示】

- 銷售本公司的新文字處理機

  ☞ *market our new word processor*

- 若有適當的地點

  ☞ *if we can find a suitable place*

- 您能提供任何資料

  ☞ *Any information you can provide*

- 爲了實現這個計畫 ☞ *get our plan started*

- 則感幸甚 ☞ *will be greatly appreciated*

秘書必備常識

Vice President 不一定是副董

■ 須以公司的組織圖判斷頭銜

Vice president 相當於我國公司中的經理一職，但美國的大企業中 Vice president 往往多達一、兩百人，有些公司甚至區分為 Senior Vice President 和 Junior Vice President 兩種階層。

至於自稱是 Vice President 的人，需經其個人解釋其地位和權利，或是由其公司的組織圖（ organization chart ）來判斷，才能與其進行實務上的交涉。僅次於董事長的副董，其英文頭銜並非 Vice President，應該是：

✗ Senior Executive Vice President

✗ Executive Vice President

Vice President 只是一般經理級的主管，譬如銷售部門經理就稱為 Vice President, Sales；製造部門經理就是 Vice President, Production。

但是，在某些公司中又表示副董，所以最好是由其本人確定或按公司組織圖加以判斷為宜。

■　在美國即使沒有下屬也可叫 manager

　　還有一項較費疑猜的頭銜，那就是 manager。有一次，台灣某家總公司在美國徵求銷售經理，結果採用了一位自稱曾任 district manager（地區經理）的人，後來才發現他原來是某地區的推銷員。在美國，只要是負責人，不論有沒有下屬都叫做 manager 。

12) 開會通知

1. 通知董事開會

【 秘書須知 】

- *There will be a meeting of ~* ☞ 舉行～之會議

- *agenda* 〔 ə'dʒɛndə 〕 *n.* 議程

- *letter of attorney* ☞ 委任書

×××××××××××××××××××× 實 例 ××××××××××××××××××××

Notice of a Directors' Meeting

To: Messrs.   Hwang

            Wu

            Wang

            Liu

            Yu

            Chen

From: Lily Wu

            Secretary

     There will be a meeting of the Board of Directors of the Sun Chemical Corporation on Tuesday, July 15th, at 1:00 p.m. at the office of corporation, 5 Chung Hsiao West Road, Taipei.

[圖] 4. 模範秘書英語書信 *175*

The research and development of the new product will be discussed.

If you cannot attend the meeting, please sign the enclosed letter of attorney and send it back to Miss Wu by the end of June.

Enclosures:　　　Agenda

　　　　　　　　　Notice of waiver

董事會議通知

致：　　　黃先生

　　　　　吳先生

　　　　　王先生

　　　　　劉先生

　　　　　余先生

　　　　　陳先生

發自：　　秘書吳莉莉

太陽化學公司董事會議將於 7 月 15 日星期二下午 1:00，假台北市忠孝西路 5 號，本公司之辦公室舉行。

會中將討論新產品的研究與發展。

如果您無法出席會議，請在隨信附寄的委任書上簽名，並於 6 月底以前交給吳小姐。

附件：　　議程

　　　　　棄權書

【註】　director〔dəˋrɛktɚ〕*n.* 董事；理事

　　　　attend〔əˋtɛnd〕*v.* 出席；參加　enclosure〔ɪnˋkloʒɚ〕*n.* 附件

　　　　waiver〔ˋwevɚ〕*n.* 棄權

2. 銷售會議通知

【 秘書須知 】

· *The last sales meeting for* **19**—*will be held on*～

☞ 19—最後一次的銷售會議，將於～舉行

✗✗✗✗✗✗✗✗✗✗✗✗✗✗✗✗✗✗ 實 例 ✗✗✗✗✗✗✗✗✗✗✗✗✗✗✗✗✗✗

Meeting Notice

To: All Salesmen

Subject: The Year-end Sales Meeting

From: Mei-mei Chen , Secretary

The last sales meeting for 19—will be held on Monday, December 17th 10:00 a.m. until 4:00 p.m. at the Head Office.

Lunch will be provided.

The agenda will be mailed by the end of November.

If you have any items to be included, please forward them to me by November 20th.

If you are unable to attend, please call 341-9403 not later than November 30th.

Thanks very much.

開　會　通　知

致：　　　所有推銷員

主題：　　年終銷售會議

發自：　　秘書陳美美

　　19—年度最後一次的銷售會議，將於 12 月 17 日，星期一上午
10 點到下午 4 點，在總公司舉行。

　　將供應午餐。

　　議程將於十一月底以前寄出。

　　如果你有任何項目欲包括在內，請於 11 月 20 日以前轉寄給我。

　　如果你無法出席，請於 11 月 30 日之前打電話至 341-9403。

　　非常謝謝。

【註】　provide〔prə'vaɪd〕*v*. 提供
　　　　item〔'aɪtəm〕*n*. 項目
　　　　forward〔'fɔrwəd〕*v*. 轉寄

~~~~~~~~~~~~~~~~~~~~~~~~~~~~~~~~~~~~~

3. 確定出席人數

【秘書須知】

· *Annual Meeting* ☞　　年度大會

· *try to estimate attendance*
　　☞　　試估出席人數

XXXXXXXXXXXXXXXXXXXXX 實例(**1**) XXXXXXXXXXXXXXXXXXXXX

To Estimate Attendance

Dear Mr. Townsend,

I hope you are still planning to attend our Annual Meeting at the Sky Building in Taipei.

We expect to start the meeting at 10:00 a.m. Since the meeting date is almost here, I am trying to estimate attendance.

I'd very much appreciate it if you could call me at 554-4167 or write to me to confirm that you are still planning to attend.

I look forward to seeing you then.

Thanks a lot,

Cordially,

....

Secretary

估計出席人數

我希望你仍然計劃出席我們在台北藍天大廈的年度會議。

我們希望會議於上午10點開始。因開會日期在卽，我正試估出席人數。

如你能打電話至 554-4167 找我或寫信給我以確定你仍然計劃出席，我將不勝感激。

屆時希望與你見面。

多謝。

【註】 appreciate〔ə'priʃı,et〕v. 感激

confirm〔kən'fɜm〕v. 證實；確定

【秘書須知】

· *Program Committee* ☞ 計劃委員會

· *To help us make adequate room and luncheon reservations*
☞ 有助於我們安排充分的空間和預訂午餐

XXXXXXXXXXXXXXXXXX **實 例(2)** XXXXXXXXXXXXXXXXX

To Estimate Attendance

To : All Branch Managers

From: Mary Hwang — Secretary

Subject: Annual Meeting

The Program Committee is making arrangements for November 16th annual meeting of the Branch Managers at 10:00 a.m. at the Sky Building in Taipei.

A program was sent to you on the 5th September.

To help us make adequate room and luncheon reservations, we would appreciate knowing whether you plan to attend the Annual Meeting this year.

For your convenience, a card is enclosed for you to indicate your intention.

Please return this card in the enclosed postage-paid envelope by October 10th.

Thank you.

估計出席人數

致： 所有分公司經理

發自： 秘書黃瑪莉

主題： 年度大會

計劃委員會正爲 11 月 16 日上午 10 點，假台北藍天大廈舉行的分公司經理年度大會做安排。

計劃將於 9 月 5 日交給您。

爲了有助於我們安排充分的空間和預訂午餐，我們將感激您讓我們知道，您是否計畫出席今年的年度大會。

爲方便您起見，附上卡片一張，以表示您的意向。

請在 10 月 10 日前，將卡片放入隨函附寄的回郵信封寄回。

謝謝您。

【註】 branch〔bræntʃ〕 *n*. 分公司；分店
　　　annual〔'ænjʊəl〕 *adj*. 一年一次的
　　　intention〔ɪn'tɛnʃən〕 *n*. 意圖；意向

EXERCISE 11

1. 湯普森先生：

　　相信您已經知道，今年度的銷售成績斐然，為了使明年也能順利成長，已準備在東京總公司召開促銷會議。

　　會議預定於5月14日星期一上午9點召開，15日下午5點閉幕，部長級、主管全體及所有上級業務員都將列席參加。

　　相信您屆時必能出席，和大家見面，談談自己的專長，增進彼此的了解。

　　附帶寄上程序表一份及總公司的詳細位置圖。

　　能否出席，幸祈儘速通知為禱。

專　　此

陳　立　源

副董事長

【提示】

- 今年度銷售成績斐然
  ☞　　*had very good sales results this year*

- 已準備召開促銷會議。
  ☞　　*be arranging a sales promotion conference*

- 部長級、主管全體 ☞　　*all our executives*

- 和大家見面 ☞　　*to meet them*

- 談談自己的專長 ☞　　*talk shop*

- 增進彼此的了解
  ☞　　*get a better understanding with each other*

- 總公司詳細位置圖
  ☞　　*a map with complete travel directions to our*
  Head Office

2.　江先生：

　　　我們非常希望您能召開促銷會議。我們知道這類會議，藉著研
討能使我們維持最近的銷售業績，同時為未來更輝煌的銷售，奠定
更緊密的合作基礎。

【提示】

- 非常希望您能召開促銷會議
  ☞　　*be very much interested to see that you are hold-*
  ing a sales promotion conference

- 這類會議
  ☞　　*a conference of this nature*

- 藉著研討能使我們維持最近良好的銷售業績
  ☞　　*a workshop will enable us to keep the latest good*
  sales results

- 為未來更輝煌的銷售，奠定更緊密的合作基礎
  ☞　　*provide a background of closer cooperation for*
  further sales promotion

秘書必備常識

Secretary of ～和 Secretary to ～有什麼不同？

在歐美的機構中，秘書是非常活躍的。舉個簡單的例子，就像你要見一位較有知名度的商場人士，就得通過秘書這一關，能否見面也得靠她決定。秘書，尤其是高級秘書，在機構中扮演上司和各往來者之間的橋樑。因此，若有人要求會面，篩選決定是秘書的責任和職權。

與國外的公司有接觸時，若給門口那位秘書不好的印象，你就難以和你想見的人會晤了，因爲她有這種權利。

還有，在秘書之後接 of 和接 to 的等級有些不同，例如：Secretary of Mr. Chen, Overseas Manager 和 Secretary to Mr. Chen, Overseas Manager 就有區別。Secretary of ～是表示在數人中當中的一個，而 Secretary to ～，則是專屬秘書，在上司面前和辦公室，具有舉足輕重的地位，其權限就要比前一種秘書大，薪水也來得多。

13) 演講邀請函

1. 請求演講

【秘書須知】

· *a ten-minute question and answer period*
  ☞　　十分鐘的問答時間

· *persons with backgrounds in marketing*
  ☞　　有行銷背景的人

· *finalize our program* ☞　　完成我們的計劃

實　例

June 18, 19—

Dear Mr. Thompson,

　　All the staff of the Central Glass Company have long admired your excellent research activities and would enjoy learning more about your work.

　　We would like to invite you to speak at the opening session of our annual seminar on Sales Promotion to be held at the Prince Hotel, Taipei, on July 9th at 10:00 a.m.

　　Since this seminar runs fifty minutes, a forty-minute address followed by a ten-minute question and answer period would be ideal.

About forty persons are expected to attend, most of them sales managers, and other persons with backgrounds in marketing.

We do hope you can join us on July 9th.

I would appreciate having your reply by July 1st so we can finalize our program.

Sincerely,

James Wu

Manager, Administration

中央玻璃公司的全體員工，長久以來一直欣賞您卓越的研究活動，並且樂於跟您多多學習，有關您的工作。

我們希望邀請您，於 7 月 9 日上午 10 點，假王子飯店舉行的年度促銷研討會的開幕中發表演講。

因爲此一研討會歷時 50 分鐘，40 分鐘演講，接著有 10 分鐘的問答時間將是理想的。

預期約有 40 人出席，大部分爲銷售經理，其他人則具有行銷背景。

我們真希望 7 月 9 日，您能和我們在一起。

我將感激您在 7 月 1 日以前答覆，以使我們的計畫得以完成。

【註】　admire〔əd'maɪr〕*v.* 欽佩；讚賞

session〔'sɛʃən〕*n.* 開會

seminar〔'sɛmə,nɑr , ,sɛmə'nɑr〕*n.* 研討會

address〔ə'drɛs〕*v.* 發表演講

2. 答應演講

【秘書須知】

· *focus on the subject of ~*   ☞   把主題訂在~

· *limit my address to forty minutes*
    ☞   將我的演講限定為40分鐘

~~~~~~~~~~~~~~~ 實 例 ~~~~~~~~~~~~~~~

Dear Mr. Wu,

It will be a pleasure to speak at the opening session of your seminar at the Prince Hotel on Tuesday, July 9th, at 10:00 a.m.

I will be glad to focus on the subject of the issue of the present-day trade friction.

As you requested, I will limit my address to forty minutes.

Your kind invitation this time is most welcome, and I'm looking forward to meeting you at the Prince Hotel.

                                    Cordially,

                                    Stephen Chao

很高興能在 7 月 9 日，上午 10 點，貴公司於王子飯店舉辦的研討會開幕中發表演講。

我將樂於把主題定在當前貿易衝突的問題上。

如您所要求的，我將演講限定爲 40 分鐘。

您這次親切的邀請，非常令人歡迎，我期待在王子飯店與您會面。

【註】　issue〔ˈɪʃʊ, ˈɪʃjʊ〕*n*. 問題

　　　　present-day〔ˈprɛzn̩tˈde〕*adj*. 當今的

　　　　friction〔ˈfrɪkʃən〕*n*. 衝突；摩擦

3. 拒絕演講

【秘書須知】

* *have a full schedule that week*
  ☞　那一週，我的時間表都已經排滿

* *Perhaps you would like to consider* ～
  ☞　或許你願意考慮

* *is well qualified to speak* ☞　非常有資格發表演講

實　例

June 25, 19—

Dear Mr. Wu,

　I am very sorry I can't accept your kind invitation to speak at the opening session of your annual seminar at the Prince Hotel on July 9th.

I have a full schedule that week.

Perhaps you would like to consider Professor Ya-nan Lee of National Taiwan University.

He is well qualified to speak, if he is free on that day.

He would be delighted to cooperate with you.

I very much regret that I can't accept your thoughtful invitation.

Thank you very much.

Sincerely,

Stephen Chao

很抱歉，我不能接受您親切的邀請，在7月9日，貴公司於王子飯店舉辦的研討會開幕中發表演講。

那一週，我的時間表都排滿。

或許您願意考慮，國立台灣大學的李亞南教授。

他非常有資格發表演講，如果他那一天有空的話。

他將樂於與您合作。

我很抱歉未能接受您慎重的邀請。

非常謝謝您。

【註】 schedule〔'skɛdʒʊl〕*n.* 時間表

thoughtful〔'θɔtfəl〕*adj.* 細心的；慎重的

EXERCISE 12

1.　　太平洋電子股份有限公司一年一度的年度會議，將於 7 月 23 日在本公司會議室舉行。

　　議題是 " Business Education and Onwards "（今後的商業教育）。我知道您在這方面至今貢獻良多，也拜讀過您在聯合報上發表的有趣文章。

　　23 日的開幕式從 10 點到 10 點半，請您務必就企業管理發表演說。

　　交通費、膳宿費由本公司支付。

　　另外支付禮金五千元。請於 7 月 1 日前告知能否參加，期待您的到來。

【提示】

・ 您在～方面貢獻良多
　☞　*you have made excellent contribution in the area of ～*

・ 在聯合報上發表的有趣文章
　☞　*the interesting article which appeared in the United Daily News*

・ 支付交通費、膳宿費
　☞　*pay your transportation, hotel and meal expenses*

・ 另外支付禮金五千元
　☞　*plus an honorarium of NT. 5000*

2. 史密斯先生：

　　　　謝謝您親切邀請本公司吳莉莉小姐，於19—年9月23日召開的秘書協會每月會議上主講。

　　　　吳小姐目前隨董事長到加拿大短期出差，下週才回國，等她回來，親自拜讀來函，再予回覆，請您放心。

【提示】

- 親切邀請
  ☞ *your gracious invitation*

- 目前隨董事長到加拿大出差
  ☞ *be now in Canada on a short business trip accompanying our President*

- 等她回來
  ☞ *on her return*

- 請您放心。
  ☞ *you can be sure that ~ .*

秘書必備常識

參加宴會應如何穿著

　　歐美人招待朋友到家舉辦宴會習以爲常，但是國人對此不太習慣，所以一旦被調任國外，最感頭疼的就是參加宴會。歐美人士除家庭式宴會外，也經常舉辦正式的大型宴會，夫婦經常相偕參加，服裝也相當講究。

▓　White Tie

　　如果邀請函的右邊寫有 White Tie 即表示這是正式的（Formal）晚宴。

　　男士穿著燕尾服（Tail Coat）、白色西裝背心，結白色領結，著黑衣鞋。女士則著晚禮服，其他如戒指、項鍊、耳環等飾物必須一應俱全，並穿著白色或銀色高跟鞋，戴白手套，提金色或銀色的串珠皮包。

▓　Black Tie

　　若邀請函右邊寫的是 Black Tie，則表示爲普通宴會，男士著無尾的半正式晚禮服（美國稱爲 Tuxedo；在英國叫做 Dinner Jacket），白襯衫，結黑領結，穿黑色皮鞋。女士則穿晚禮服，其他則與正式宴會無異。

　　有些邀請卡不寫 White Tie 或者 Black Tie，而寫 Formal、Informal，意思都是一樣的。若寫 Business Attire 的話，則是極爲普通的宴會。男士著質料格調較高雅的暗色西裝（business suit），女士可穿午宴服，但男女雙方都應穿無帶皮鞋。

14) 疾病慰問函

1. 意外事件慰問函

【秘書須知】

· ***but equally relieved to learn that ~***
  ☞ 但得知~同樣地鬆了一口氣

· ***received many orders*** ☞ 接到許多訂單

· ***newly-developed word processor***
  ☞ 新開發的文字處理機

· ***With modern facilities at ~*** ☞ 由於~的現代化設備

✿✿✿✿✿✿✿✿✿✿✿✿✿✿ **實 例** ✿✿✿✿✿✿✿✿✿✿✿✿✿✿

October 9, 19—

Dear Mr. Hwang,

I was very sorry to hear when I called at your office today, that you had been in the Hsin Hai Tunnel Car Accident, but equally relieved to learn that you are now making satisfactory progress in the City Hospital.

In a long talk with Miss Lee, your secretary, I was told business is quite good and your company has received many orders for your newly-developed word processor.

✿ 　　　With modern facilities at the City Hospital, you will
✿ be all right and back in your office again very soon.
✿ 　　　I am sending you some flowers and a little fruit,
✿ with my sincere wishes for your quick recovery.

　　　　　　　　　　　Yours sincerely,

　　　　　　　　　　　...................

　　　　　　　　　　　Manager of Administration

　　今天當我拜訪您的辦公室，聽到您在辛亥隧道發生車禍時，感到
非常難過，但是得知您現今在市立醫院的進步很令人滿意，同樣地鬆
了一口氣。

　　在和您的秘書李小姐的長談中，她告訴我業務相當順利，貴公司
接到許多新開發的文字處理機的訂單。

　　由於市立醫院的現代化設備，您將很快地好轉，再度回到辦公室。

　　我送您一些鮮花和水果，並誠摯地祝福您早日康復。

✦　　　　　　✦　　　　　　✦

【註】　tunnel〔ˈtʌn!〕*n*. 隧道

　　　　satisfactory〔ˌsætɪsˈfæktərɪ〕*adj*. 令人滿意的

秘書必備常識

I am a martini drinker （我喜歡喝馬丁尼）

▓ 安排商業午餐是秘書的職責

I am a martini drinker.除了「我喜歡喝馬丁尼」之外，尚有誇示自己是具有動用交際費（*expense account*）地位的重要人物。通常洽談商務大多數選擇午餐時間，邊喝酒邊吃牛排，稱爲 Business Lunch（商業午餐）。

代替上司和客戶約定商業午餐的時間和地點，爲上司和客戶製造舒適寧靜的洽談機會，是秘書的手腕之一。從一杯雞尾酒達到圓滿交易結果並非癡人說夢。

▓ 餐會前三天到一個星期就要連絡安排

歐美人士用餐時，特別是到高級的餐廳，絕對不喝啤酒，所以要是忽略了這一點，而請外國客戶喝啤酒，這必會給對方極不好的印象，因爲歐美人士認爲啤酒是代替開水的飲料，不宜在餐廳飲用。

到高級餐廳用餐，首先持一杯白蘭地，用手掌的溫度暖酒，品嚐著它的香味，一邊洽談。到用餐時則要點其他酒或雞尾酒，最具代表性的是馬丁尼。

要請客戶用餐時，需在三天至一個星期前連絡、安排。這時，若告訴對方 Let's have lunch together（我們一道吃午餐），可能被誤解爲 Let's go Dutch （我們平均分攤吧），爲更明白清楚起見，最好是用 I would like you to be our guest at ~on Tuesday, 17th October. （我希望10月17日，星期二能請你吃飯）的說法，這樣才算是稱職的秘書。

15) 死亡通知、弔唁函

1. 董事長死亡通知函

【秘書須知】

- *the Board of Directors* ☞ 董事會
- *announce with deep sorrow* ☞ 懷著深深的哀傷宣告

實　例

The Board of Directors, Far East Glass Co., Ltd., announce with deep sorrow the sudden death of their president Nai-hsin Lu on the afternoon of July 16th, 19—.

遠東玻璃有限公司董事會懷著深深的哀傷宣告，董事長呂乃信在 19—年7月16日下午溘然長逝。

✦　　　✦　　　✦

【註】　sudden〔'sʌdn̩〕 *adj.* 突然的
　　　　president〔'prɛzədənt〕 *n.* 董事長

2. 副董事長死亡的通知函

【秘書須知】

- *Senior Executive Vice-President* ☞ 副董事長
- *funeral service* ☞ 葬禮

實 例

With deep grief we have to announce the death of Kang Lee, Senior Executive Vice-President of our Company.

He died at National Taiwan University Hospital on the morning of December 23rd, 19—.

The funeral service will be held at 2:00 p.m. Thursday, December 25th, 19—, at Municipal Funeral Parlor, Taipei.

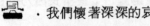

- 我們懷著深深的哀傷，宣告敝公司副董事長，李剛的去世。

他在19—年12月23日早上，死於台大醫院。

葬禮將在19—年12月25日，星期四下午兩點，假台北市立殯儀館舉行。

【註】 announce〔ə'naʊns〕v. 公布；宣告
Municipal Funeral Parlor 市立殯儀館

3. 弔唁函

【秘書須知】

- *be distressed to read ～ = be deeply grieved to read ～*
  ☞　看到～感到很悲痛

- *express one's deep regret*　☞　表達某人深沈的惋惜

- *untimely passing = untimely death*　☞　早死；夭折

- *extend our deepest pity and hearty condolence*
  ☞　表示我們最深沈的同情和衷心的慰問

- *his bereaved family*　☞　遺族

〰〰〰〰〰〰〰〰〰〰〰〰〰〰〰　實　例　〰〰〰〰〰〰〰〰〰〰〰〰〰〰〰

April 5, 19—

Dear Mr. White,

　　We were distressed to read the announcement of Mr. Smith's death in this morning's Central Daily News, and write immediately to express our deep regret.

　　By his untimely passing the camera industry has lost one of its pioneers.

　　We recall his great kindness and active cooperation with our company in the past.

　　He will long be remembered by all who knew him and who worked with him.

On behalf of our company, please extend our deepest pity and hearty condolence to his bereaved family.

Yours very sincerely,

....

今天早晨，我們看到中央日報上史密斯先生的訃聞，感到非常悲痛，立刻寫這封信，以表我們深深的惋惜。

由於史密斯先生不幸早逝，照相機工業喪失了一名開拓者。

我們憶起過去他那無比的親切，以及和本公司積極地合作。

所有認識他的人以及和他共事者，將永遠記得他。

請代表本公司，向史密斯先生的遺族，表示我們最深沈的同情和衷心的慰問。

＊　　　　＊　　　　＊

【註】 announcement〔ə'naʊnsmənt〕*n.* 布告；訃聞
　　　 pioneer〔,paɪə'nɪr〕*n.* 先驅者；拓荒者
　　　 recall〔rɪ'kɔl〕*v.* 記起；召回　　active〔'æktɪv〕*adj.* 主動的；積極的
　　　 cooperation〔ko,ɑpə'reʃən〕*n.* 合作；協力

秘書必備常識

R.S.V.P.知多少？

　　這可不是白蘭地的名稱哦！是寫在邀請函下面的文字。最近國內有許多公司舉辦活動時亦以英文邀請函的姿態出現。在此，特就R.S.V.P.做一番說明。這是採自法文Répondez s'il vous plaît（敬請回覆）這個句子的第一個字母構成的。

　　歐、美小學四年級左右的孩子就已懂得R.S.V.P.的意義。若R.S.V.P.下寫有電話號碼時，即表示以電話回覆之意；若R.S.V.P.下接President's Office就是向董事長室回覆；若爲Secretary就是向秘書回覆的意思。

　　若受到邀請而未能參加時，如果時間上允許，最好都能以書面回覆。正式的回信，主詞不用I、we，而用he、she、they，非正式信件當然就無此限制了。

第**5**章

秘書接待英語

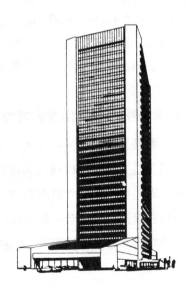

1) 秘書接待態度

對於來訪客人的接待方式及禮節稱為應對。當妳正在打字時，若有客人進來說到 " Excuse me. " 或 " Good morning. " 時，單單把頭轉向客人，或是雙手插腰，或雙臂環抱於胸前等姿勢，都會給予對方很不好的印象。以下舉出各基本要點，可為接待外國客戶時的參考：

(1) 立刻接待客人

尤其是 receptionist secretary (接待秘書) 應該經常保持馬上可以接待客人的姿勢，即使在接電話，也應機警地面向客人，以眼神打招呼。

(2) 親切、微笑地打招呼

招呼的方式可用 " Good morning, sir. " 或 " Good afternoon, ma'am. " 若是已認識的人，可以 Mr. Jackson, Mrs. Adams等稱呼代替 sir 及 ma'am。因為稱呼名字顯得較親切。

在打招呼時，應輕輕點頭並面帶微笑，不必握手。

(3) 交談時需適當地注視對方的眼睛

雖然東南亞人、非洲人、美國黑人、波多黎各人為表示恭敬時都是雙目下垂，但是，白種人對這種行為大多會認為不夠大方、磊落，相反地，若是目不轉睛地盯著對方，可能被誤會為別有愛意 (阿拉伯人例外)，所以在談到重點，告一段落或回答 Yes、No 時應該注視對方的眼睛，其他時候不必刻意注視對方眼睛。

(4) 不熟悉的客人來訪時，務必問清其姓名及所屬團體

"May I have your name, please?"是最普通的用法。詢問其公司名稱時，可用"What company are you from?"或"What company do you represent?"，更鄭重的用法是"Could you tell me what company you are representing?"

(5) 必須用雙手把對方名片接過來

各國訪客中大概以日本人最常交換名片，其他各國人也偶有這種習慣，秘書在接過名片時，務必雙手接過以示尊重，同時，接過手後不要隨手玩弄或棄置桌面。想要對方名片時可說"Would you give me your business card?"，拿到名片後必須問"Mr. Alexander J. Hughes of Western Electric Co.?" "Is your name pronounced〔hjuz〕?"以示確認，若不太清楚如何發音時，不要隨便亂唸，應詢問"How do you pronounce your last name, please?"為宜。

(6) 有客人未事先約定而來訪時，不要直接回答他上司在與不在

"May I see Mr. Chen?" "Is Mr. Williams in?"之類沒有事先約定就上門造訪的客人，不必直接回答他"Yes"或"No"，可先以"I'll see if he is available."加以搪塞，然後再以"May I tell him what you wish to see him about?"詢問來意，但是，不要對看來重要的客人多次詢問。不論碰到多麼複雜的情況，還是要冷靜、沉著的應付，儘量從來者回答的情報中，充分判斷是否需要讓他與上司見面。

(7) 清晰鑑定來客的種類

像以下的各種訪客，您應按情況判斷是否能引見，或是何者優先。
ⓐ客戶　　ⓑ工作上的伙伴（加入團體或業界的伙伴）
ⓒ家人，親戚　　ⓓ個人的好友　　ⓔ其他人

　　還要考慮這些事情緊急與否，是否有事先約定。在上列名單當中客戶自然是居於最優先的地位，但還是應該以其緊急的程度及來意做判斷。至於ⓒ的家人、親戚，尤其是親戚，應該要幫他轉達，再由主管自己決定。而像ⓔ這類不認識的訪客，若事先有約定或持有介紹信時，也不能怠慢了才好。

⑻ 不論什麼客人，都應以公平、鄭重且毅然的態度接待之。

　　即使是ⓔ等不熟悉之客人，且沒有事先約定，也不能改變親切的態度，萬一需要拒絕會晤，亦需陳述原由，如 "I'm sorry, Mr. Chen has a full schedule this week. Could you please write a note to him on the matter you wish to see him about?" 免得讓對方太難堪。

　　但是，萬一他要威脅上司或硬要闖入，秘書可毫不客氣予以拒絕："I'm sorry, but Mr. Chen cannot see you." 若他無視於秘書的拒絕而強行進入的話，秘書得以緊急鈴聲等請求救援。

⑼ 沒有上司確切答覆，不能擅自予以引見

　　預先約定的訪客，秘書自當報告上司 "Mr. Chen, Mr. Baker is here for his three o'clock appointment."，若是沒有事先約定，而秘書判斷是百分之百可以會見的客人，也不能擅作決定，應先請示主管。

⑽ 上司不在又無法聯絡時有重要客人來訪，需告知必與其連絡：

　　譬如，可以用 "I'm sorry, he's not in now. Shall I have him call you when he returns?"，若對方回答 "Yes, please." 並告訴妳連絡地址、電話時，妳必須附帶問一下打電話的時間許可範圍，如 "Can he call you in the afternoon?"

⑾表示請對方稍等時

可用 " Would you please have a seat and wait for a few moments？" 或 " Would you like to sit down, Mr. Wilson？"一邊指示座位，並準備雜誌給客人看，但是，不必陪他們聊天。然後，回到較遠的座位辦自己的事。離開座位時，須謹防客人看到桌上的文件。

⑿ 帶領客人做介紹時，要走在客人前方2～3步做引導。

先說 " Would you come this way, please？" 而後自己先走，客人自然就會跟著你走。若遇轉角時，先停下來指示方向 " This way, please." 然後才開始繼續走。

⒀ 搭乘電梯時，應該讓客人先上或先下

上電梯時按下按鈕，待電梯門開後，可對客人說 " Would you get on the elevator, please？"，同樣地，下電梯時，也要說 " Would you step out, please？" 待客人下後，自己再下。

⒁ 開鎖門時，左右手呈交叉，不可面向後方。

也就是說門把在左，就用右手開，在右則用左手開，這種姿勢較優美。若是向內推的門，自己應先進去，拉住門，再說 " Would you come in, please？"，請客人入內。

⒂ 請對方就會客室的上座

通常一邊說 " Please have a seat, Mr. Jones . Mr. Smith will see you in a few minutes." 一邊請對方就首席。一般來說，會客室的首席位置都是如下一頁圖所示，距離入口最遠的沙發。

會客室座席順序

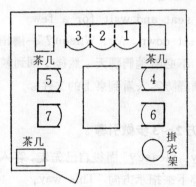
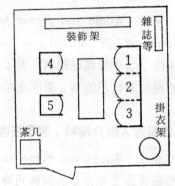

(16) 若長時間等候，不應該就任其獨坐

　　秘書固然沒有陪訪客聊天的義務，但若讓對方久等時，應該偶爾向對方說明 "I'm sorry to have to keep you waiting, but he's still not free."，並且應多準備一些報章雜誌供訪客消磨時間。

(17) 有外國訪客前來，準備飲料時應詢問對方之好惡

　　國內客戶來訪，可直接倒茶招待，但若外國訪客，由於習慣之差異，最好詢問對方偏好，如 "Would you like coffee or tea?" "How do you like your coffee?" 等，這是禮貌，雖然有些外國人也挺喜歡中國茶的。

(18) 對於和上司初次見面的訪客，秘書應該簡單地介紹一下

　　對有約定的客戶，秘書向上司報告時說 "Mr. Chen, Mr. Baker is here." 就可以了。但是，按情況可有所變通。例如，上司比訪客地位高時，就說 "Mr. Chen, this is Mr. Baker of the Atlantic Corporation." 相反地，若Mr. Baker 地位較高時，則用 "Mr. Baker, this is Mr. Chen."；若爲男性與女性，則以女士優先。

⒆ **若必須與正在和客人談話的上司聯絡時，應以書面呈示**

　　有事稟明正和客人談話的上司時，應先做成書面報告，或帶著突然造訪的訪客名片進入會客室，首先向客人道歉 " Excuse me for interrupting. "，然後呈示上司，靜候上司回覆，退出時，應禮貌地再次抱歉 " I'm sorry to have interrupted you. "

⒇ **客人臨走前必須鄭重地道別**

　　就是再忙也別忘了最後的道別。直接稱呼名字，如 " Good-bye, Mr. Baker. " 容易給人較好的印象。就是初次來訪的客人也要想法記住其姓名。

⒇ **作成來訪者卡片**

　　作成寫有姓名、團體、職位、地址、電話、來意、訪問日期、特徵等的個別卡片，按字母順序或其他條件予以分類，一方面可做爲下次訪問時間的參考，也可促成彼此間更好的溝通。

2) 秘書接待實例

a. 接待員用

　　做爲一個成功的 receptionist - secretary, 應當怎樣與客人應對？以下舉一實例供讀者參考。此外，若能詳記「秘書接待須知」並加以活用，更是相得益彰

【 *秘書接待須知* 】

・ *May I help you* ? ☞　　我能爲您服務嗎？

・ *May I have your name, please* ? ☞　　請問尊姓大名？

- **This is reception.**

  ☞　　這是接待處。（用於以電話傳達時。）

- **Mr. Smith is here for his appointment.**

  ☞　　史密斯先生來此赴約。

實　例

Receptionist :　Good morning, may I help you?

　　　　　　　　早安，我能爲您服務嗎？

Visitor :　Yes, I have an appointment with Mr.
Chen, the vice-president.

　　　　　　可以的，我和陳副董事長約了時間見面。

Receptionist :　May I have your name, please?

　　　　　　　　請問尊姓大名？

Visitor :　George Smith of Walsh Company.

　　　　　　我是華爾希公司的喬治・史密斯。

Receptionist :　Thank you very much, Mr. Smith. I'll
call Mr. Chen's office.

　　　　　　　　非常謝謝您，史密斯先生。我會打電話到
陳先生的辦公室。

Receptionist :　（以內線電話）Mr. Chen's office? This
is reception. Mr. George Smith of
Walsh Company is here for his appointment. 陳先生的辦公室嗎？這是接待
處。華爾希公司的喬治・史密斯先生，來
此赴約。

Secretary : （以內線電話）Please send him up.

請他上來。

Receptionist : Thank you. 謝謝您。

Receptionist : （對客人說）Mr. Chen is expecting you,
Mr. Smith. Please take the elevator on
your right to the fifth floor. Mr.
Chen's office is No. 505, on the left.

史密斯先生，陳先生正在恭候大駕。請乘
在你右邊的電梯到五樓。陳先生的辦公室
在左邊，505 號。

Visitor : Thank you very much. 非常謝謝妳。

Receptionist : You're welcome. 不客氣。

b. 對有約定的常客

秘書對有約定的訪客，應立卽通知上司安排會面,若爲熟悉的訪客，
可加上 "How are you？" 等應對之詞，這是爲上司維繫圓滿的人際關
係，值得注意之處。同時要注意到，非常誠懇、親切地稱呼對方的名字，
這種小節也是良好交際上，萬萬不可忽略的地方。

【秘書接待須知】

· *I'll tell Mr. Chen that you're here.*

☞　　我會轉告陳先生您來了。

· *Please go right in.* ☞　　請進。

實 例

Visitor : Hello, Ms. Wu, how are you today?

嗨，吳小姐，今天怎麼樣？

Secretary : Fine, thank you, Mr. Smith. How have you been?

很好，謝謝你，史密斯先生。最近如何？

Visitor : Just fine. 還不錯。

Secretary : Mr. Chen is expecting you. I'll tell him that you're here.

陳先生正恭候大駕。我會轉告他您來了。

（以內線電話）Mr. Chen, Mr. Smith is here. 陳先生，史密斯先生來了。

Mr. Chen : Send him in. 請他進來。

Secretary : Yes, Mr. Chen. 好的，陳先生。

（對客人）Please go right in. 請進。

c. 沒有約定的常客

　　秘書應以上司之方便爲優先條件，若有不速之客，應加以詢問，判斷輕重再決定是否要稟明上司。但若是重要客戶，一再詢問似乎有欠禮貌，所以應該立即向上司轉達，以確定意向。像以下實例這種緊急事件，用內線電話並無不妥，但依情況而定，有時應直接到上司辦公室報告。

【秘書接待須知】

· *Let me see if he is available.*

☞　我看看他是否方便。

· *Mr. Chen is occupied at the moment.*

☞　陳先生現在正在忙。

· *Mr. Chen wants to know if your business is urgent.*

☞　陳先生想知道您的事急不急。

· *Would you please have a seat and wait for a moment?*

☞　請您坐著等一下好嗎？

━━━ **實　例** ━━━

Visitor ： Good afternoon, Ms. Lee. I'd like to see Mr. Chen for a few minutes, if I could.
午安，李小姐。如果可以的話，我想見陳先生幾分鐘。

Secretary ： Nice to see you, Mr. Lawson. Let me see if he is available. Would you wait just a moment, please? 幸會，洛遜先生。我看看他是否方便。請稍候。

（用內線電話）Mr. Chen, Mr. Lawson is here and would like to see you for a few moments. 陳先生，洛遜先生來了，希望和您見面一會兒。

Chen : I'm busy right now. Would you find out what he wants to see me about?

我現在很忙。麻煩妳問他有何貴幹?

Secretary : Certainly, Mr. Chen. (對客人) Mr. Chen is occupied at the moment and wants to know if your business is urgent.

好的,陳先生。陳先生現在正在忙。他想知道您的事急不急。

Visitor : Well, I've found a problem in the contract he asked me to examine yesterday. He told me that it was an urgent matter.

嗯,昨天他叫我審查的合同中,我發現一個問題。他告訴我那是緊急事件。

Secretary : I see. Let me ask him again. Would you please have a seat and wait for a moment?

我明白了。讓我再問問看。請您坐著等一下,好嗎?

Visitor : Thank you. 謝謝妳。

Secretary : (用內線電話) Mr. Chen, Mr. Lawson says that he has found a problem in the contract you asked him to look at yesterday.

陳先生,洛遜先生說,他在你昨天叫他審查的合同中,發現了一個問題。

> Chen： I see. Well, that is important. Ask him
> to come in.
> 原來如此。嗯，那很要緊。請他進來。
> Secretary： All right, Mr. Chen.（對客人）Please go
> right in. 好的，陳先生。請進。
> Visitor： Thank you. 謝謝妳。

d. 初次約定會面的客人

若是有約定的客人，其要領大致同於 b，但由於是初次來訪，應帶領至上司辦公室，簡單地向上司介紹。

【 秘書接待須知 】

. **Mr. Chen can see you now.**
　☞　　陳先生馬上可以見您。

. **Would you come this way, please？**
　☞　　請往這兒走。

實　例

> Visitor： Good afternoon. I have an appointment
> with Mr. Chen for 2:00.
> 午安，我和陳先生約好了兩點鐘見面。
> Secretary： Are you Mr. Roth of Best Foods？
> 您是優佳食品的羅斯先生嗎？

Visitor : Yes, that's right. 正是。

Secretary : I'll tell Mr. Chen that you're here.
Would you like to have a seat over there
for a moment, please?

我會轉告陳先生，您來了。請您在那兒坐一
下好嗎？

Visitor : Thank you. 謝謝您

Secretary : （用內線電話）Mr. Chen, Mr. Roth of
Best Foods is here for his 2 o'clock
appointment.

陳先生，優佳食品的羅斯先生來此赴兩點的
約會。

Chen : Send him in, please. 請他進來。

Secretary : Yes, Mr. Chen. （對客人）Mr. Chen can
see you now, Mr. Roth. Would you come
this way, please? （對客人）Mr. Chen,
this is Mr. Roth of Best Foods.

好的，陳先生。羅斯先生，陳先生馬上可以
見您。請往這兒走。陳先生，這位是優佳食
品的羅斯先生。

e. 初次相見，又沒有事先約定的客人

這類客人是最令人頭疼的，以下所舉的是一段親切，鄭重又果決的
秘書應對實例。讀者不難注意到，這個實例中，雖然上司的回答是 "Not

interested." 但是，秘書還是委婉告訴對方，「有機會再聯絡」。

【秘書接待須知】

- *Do you have an appointment*?　☞　　您預先約定了嗎？

- *Can I ask what you wish to see him about*?
  ☞　　請問您有什麼事要見他？

- *I'm told to get that information from every caller*.
  ☞　　我奉命詢問每位訪客的來意。（這裏的 information 是 指來意）

- *Would you please leave your card*?
  ☞　　請您留下名片好嗎？（leave 用於離開時，一般則以 give me 較常用。）

—————— 實　例 ——————

　　Visitor :　Hello, I'd like to see Mr. Chen, please.
　　　　　　　嗨，我想和陳先生見個面，麻煩妳。

　Secretary :　Do you have an appointment?
　　　　　　　您預先約定了嗎？

　　Visitor :　No, I don't, but I'll take just a few
　　　　　　　minutes of his time.
　　　　　　　沒有，但是我祇花他幾分鐘的時間。

　Secretary :　Can I have your name, please?
　　　　　　　請問您尊姓大名？

Visitor : My name is Henry Wilkins.

我是亨利‧威爾金斯。

Secretary : And can I ask what you wish to see him about?

請問您有什麼事要見他？

Visitor : I'd prefer to explain that to him directly. 我比較喜歡直接向他說明。

Secretary : I'm sorry, but I'm told to get that information from every caller.

抱歉，我奉命詢問每位訪客的來意。

Visitor : I see. Well, I'm from International Lease Corporation and I was wondering if he is interested in leasing cars from us.

原來如此。嗯，我來自國際租貸公司，我想知道他對向我們租車子，是否感興趣？

Secretary : I see. Just a moment, please.

我明白了，請等一下。

Secretary : （用內線電話）Mr. Chen, Mr. Henry Wilkins of the International Lease Corporation is here to see you. He wants to know if you want to lease cars.

陳先生，國際租貸公司的亨利‧威爾金斯先生來此想見您。他想知道您是否想租車子。

Chen : Not interested. 沒興趣。

Secretary : I see. （對客人）I'm sorry, but Mr. Chen says that he is not interested in leasing cars at the moment but that he may want to get in touch with you in the future. Would you please leave your card?

知道了。抱歉，陳先生說，目前他對租車子尚不感興趣，但是將來可能會跟您聯絡，請您留下名片好嗎？

Visitor : All right. Here you are. 好的。這個就是。

Secretary : Thank you. Good-by. 謝謝您，再見。

3) 秘書接待自我測驗

針對前面兩個部分的應用，以下是幾個實況會話測驗，請自行試做再參考解答。

● 自我測驗 1

您是陳副董事長的秘書，現在時刻是 13 點 55 分，客戶 Starlight Foods Company 的代表 Mr. Rollins 來赴兩點的約會，身為秘書的您，該如何接待呢？

Mr. Rollins : Hello, Ms. Chao.

Secretary : (1)＿＿＿＿＿＿＿＿＿＿＿

Mr. Rollins : Fine, thank you. Is Mr. Chen in?

Secretary : (2)＿＿＿＿＿＿＿＿＿＿＿

（用內線電話對上司說）(3)＿＿＿＿＿＿＿＿＿

Mr. Chen : Send him in.

Secretary : (4)＿＿＿＿＿＿＿＿＿＿＿

（Mr. Rollins）(5)＿＿＿＿＿＿＿＿＿

Mr. Rollins : Thank you.

解　答

(1) Hello, Mr. Rollins, how are you?

(2) Yes, he's expecting you. I'll tell him you're here.

(3) Mr. Chen, Mr. Rollins is here for his 2 o'clock appointment.

(4) All right, Mr. Chen.

(5) Please go right in.

● 自我測驗 2

　　11 點時有約定的 Mr. Page 按時前來，但是陳副董尚未回公司。您該怎麼應對呢？

Mr. Page : Hello, Ms. Chao. Can I see Mr. Chen now?

Secretary : (1)＿＿＿＿＿＿＿＿＿＿＿

Mr. Page ： Thank you.

過了十分鐘副董還未回來，所以秘書打電話詢問，確定他已在回程中，所以對 Mr. Page 說：

Secretary ： (2)＿＿＿＿＿＿＿＿＿＿＿＿＿＿＿＿＿＿
Mr. Page ： That's all right.

解　答

(1) How do you do, Mr. Page? Mr. Chen is out of the office at the moment but I expect him back shortly. Won't you please have a seat over there for a few moments?

(2) I'm sorry to have kept you waiting, Mr. Page. Mr. Chen is on his way back, so he should be here any minute. Thank you for waiting.

【注意】若上司將要晚一點回來時，應詢問對方是否願意多等一會兒。要是不得不請對方先回去，應該慎重表示歉意，並告知上司回來一定馬上以電話跟他聯絡。

　　客人在等候時，應有的服務是倒茶，請對方看些書報雜誌，甚至偶爾和他說說話，以減輕其焦急情緒。

● **自我測驗 3**

上司陳副董在辦公室與張副董洽談。兩人就草莓果醬的滯銷，庫存過剩討論了三十分鐘。這時，客戶貿易商江先生無約定而來訪，您該怎麼處理？

Mr. Chiang： Good morning, Ms. Chao.

Secretary ： (1)＿＿＿＿＿＿＿＿＿＿＿＿＿＿＿＿

Mr. Chiang： Fine, Thanks. I'd like to see Mr. Chen for a few minutes, please.

Secretary ： (2)＿＿＿＿＿＿＿＿＿＿＿＿＿＿＿＿

Mr. Chiang： Yes, I've got to have 500 cases of strawberry jam as soon as possible and I was hoping that Pacific had some.

Secretary ： (3)＿＿＿＿＿＿＿＿＿＿＿.＿＿＿＿＿

（以書面向上司呈遞江先生的來意，並靜候指示）

(4)＿＿＿＿＿＿＿＿＿＿＿＿＿＿＿＿

Chen ： Wonderful！Send him in right away.

(5)＿＿＿＿＿＿＿＿＿＿＿＿＿＿＿＿

（對江先生說）(6)＿＿＿＿＿＿＿＿＿＿＿

Mr. Chiang： Thanks very much.

實　例

(1) Good morning, Mr. Chiang. How are you today？

(2) I'm afraid he's in conference right now. Can I ask what you wish to see him about?

(3) I see. Let me take him a note. Would you have a seat over there for a moment, please?

(4) Excuse me for interrupting, but you have a visitor, Mr. Chen.

(5) Certainly, Mr. Chen.

(6) Mr. Chiang, Mr. Chen can see you now. Please go in.

【注意】如果此事如上例這樣圓滿解決,秘書就可以省掉許多麻煩,但在實際情況與此相距甚遠。這類事情大多複雜難以處理,若事關重大,不論情況如何都應該沉著應付,呈報上司等候指示。如例所示,即使對上司討論的事項有了解,也不應該在(3)處說"That's wonderful. We were trying to sell our strawberry jam."到了上司辦公室不一定要以書面請示,只說"Mr. Chiang is here and he wants to buy 500 cases of strawberry jam."就可以了。所以可以實際情況如何,做各種行事判斷。

● 自我測驗 4

有位陌生的訪客進門說道"Has Mr. Chen left for the New Century Hotel?",上司是馬上就要到新世紀飯店,知道這事的人,必是和老闆極爲熟悉的人,您該怎麼辦?

Visitor : Hello. Has Mr. Chen left for the New Century Hotel?

Secretary : (1)_____

Visitor ： Oh, I'm a member of the Press Club. I'd like to see him just for a second.

Secretary ： (2) _____

Visitor ： I'd rather speak to him personally.

Secretary ： (3) _____

Visitor ： I see. I'm from the Central Daily News. I hear that Mr. Chen is a good friend of Mr. Spencer, the Executive Managing Director of WBM Co., and am wondering if I could talk to him just a little about the WBM case, maybe in his car, on the way to the hotel.

Secretary ： (4) _____

Visitor ： All right. Here's my business card. My name is pronounced〔ˈstivənz〕

Secretary ： (5) _____

Visitor ： Thank you.

Secretary ： （進上司辦公室對他說）

(6) _____

Chen ： Humm.... Please tell him that I'm going to the hotel with someone else and can't talk to him in the car, and that, if he wants to see me, he should ask for an appointment in advance.

Secretary ： (7) _____

（對 Mr. Stephens 說）(8) _____

Visitor ： How about tomorrow morning ?

Secretary ： (9) _____

Visitor ： That's too bad. Well, I'll call you some other time, then.

Secretary ： (10) _____

解 答

(1) May I have your name, please?

(2) May I tell him what you wish to see him about?

(3) I'm sorry but I'm told to ask all visitors what they wish to see him about, so I have to get that information from every caller.

(4) I see. Would you give me your business card?

(5) Thank you, Mr. Stephens. I'll tell him that you are here.

(6) Mr. Chen, Mr. Stephens of the Central Daily News is here. He wants to talk with you about Mr. Spencer of WBM, and is wondering if you could talk with him in your car going to the New Century Hotel.

(7) All right, Mr. Chen.

(8) I'm sorry, but Mr. Chen is going to the hotel with someone else, and cannot talk to you. Could you make an appointment on some other day?

(9) I'm afraid Mr. Chen has a full day tomorrow.

(10) Thank you very much. Good-bye.

【注意】千萬別因為客人的第一句話就上當，若馬上告訴他 "Not yet." 就糟了。應該先不回答在或不在，而詢問對方姓名、來意，如果對方不願告訴你，至少要弄清楚對方是何許人。

秘書必備常識

宴會中的飲酒常識

■ **不可自己倒酒**

　　在宴會場合，中國人喜歡自己倒酒，或彼此為對方倒酒，認為這是增進彼此情誼的方式之一。但是西方社會，切記不要有這樣的舉動，歐美人士都是由主人或侍者進行這項工作，所以當你參加歐美人士的宴席，千萬別僭奪了主人或侍者的職稱，特別注意，這也是自貶身價的行為。

■ **別人替你斟酒時，不要將杯子拿起來**

　　還有一點要提醒各位的是，參加非正式的宴會或雞尾酒會時，由於會場中侍者人數不足，忙不過來，可以相互斟酒。但是為別人斟酒時，絕不可以讓對方持著空杯讓你斟酒，這是非常不禮貌的，應該將對方的杯子接過來，斟完後再交給對方。若是主人或侍者來替你斟酒時，不必將杯子從桌上拿起來便於對方倒酒。因為這種舉動會給外國人乞食的感覺。只要好好坐著，不必動手。

第**6**章

秘書翻譯對策

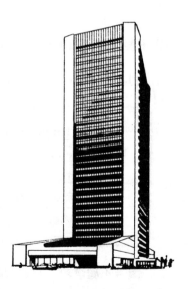

1) 秘書翻譯技巧

就技術分類而言，翻譯的方法可區分爲三種：

ad hoc interpreting 特　別　翻　譯	少數人討論時的翻譯法。
consecutive interpreting 逐　次　翻　譯	演講時面對衆人，分成一部分、一部分地翻譯主講人的話。
simultaneous interpreting 同　步　翻　譯	不是逐次地，而是將說話者的話，同時翻譯出來。

秘書雖然不是翻譯專家，但是偶而也要爲賓客、外國上司或外國客戶與老闆之間翻譯。在以上三種情形中，以第一種情況所佔的比例最高，以下是在做這種翻譯時，應把握的訣竅：

(1) 不要摻雜主觀想法或加以誇大

初次擔任翻譯時，很容易犯以下的毛病：

> " I think he means that the delay is being caused
> by tremendous difficulty in dealing with the opposi-
> tion of the local residents. "
> 　我認爲他的意見是說，拖延是由於處理當地居民的反對，
> 有極大的困難。

讀者不難發現，其實劃線的部分是不需要的。當然，也不能隨意省略或歪曲了內容，這些都是翻譯時應具備的基本態度與素養。

(2) 做筆記

簡易的內容雖不必如此，但是做筆記並不見得會聽漏說話者的重點，因此，最好還是準備一下筆記簿，遇到中翻英時，就以英語做紀錄，英翻中時就以中文記下關鍵字，這樣可使翻譯時減少困難，也可使用一些記號，以免遺漏掉重點或者內容，例如：

"What you told me yesterday was just fine. What I'm concerned about is whether this is the right time to get it started. Roy Chao tells me that the failure of A & M was mainly due to the lack of support of the people who live in that area. So, I think we should take some more time to pave the way in that connection."

你昨天告訴我的很不錯。我擔心的是，現在就開始，是不是合宜的時機。趙羅伊跟我說，A＆M的失敗，大部分歸因於缺乏當地居民的支持。因此，我認為，我們應該多花點時間為此鋪路。

這裏，筆記可記為：

昨 ♡ ok →

擔心 → start

Roy ♡ A & M fail 住民的支持 ✕

∴ ＝ pave ①

　　這兒口的記號代表「talk」,往下彎曲的箭頭是躊躇,「可是」之意。∴表「所以」,兩道平行線表地平線,即「道路」之意,時鐘表「時間」。這是一次 consecutive interpreting (逐次翻譯)時的紀錄,對於少數人討論時的翻譯,極有助益。

⑶ 爲了節省時間,必需使用同時翻譯的技巧

　　通常,正規的同時翻譯用在較大型的場合,外賓每需戴上小型耳機,從耳機接收翻譯員的譯文。但是,在小型的討論會中,有時也用同時翻譯的技巧(就是將話直接傳於聽者耳朵的 whispering 的方式)。英文能力強的秘書,可用這種方法翻譯,以節省時間。不過,必須注意的是,對於技術性或者密度較高的內容,由於時間的限制,可能祇能表達 80%,相當有局限性。

　　在這兒,同時將翻譯的結構與技巧,以圖表示出來。

　　首先,談逐次翻譯的結構:

Speaker　　　Speaking
(說話者)　　　　(說)

Interpreter　Listening → Decoding → Encoding →
(翻譯者)　　　(聽)　　　(譯解)　　(將印象
　　　　　　　　　　　　　　　　　　記號化)

　　　　　　　　Speaking →
　　　　　　　　(說出來)

　　原則上，同步翻譯是 listening 和 speaking 同時進行，但是如果不聽完說話者講到一個段落，也無法翻譯，其次，在譯出的同時，還得豎起耳朵注意下一部分（即下圖所示）。

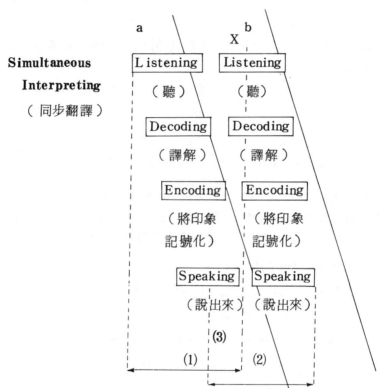

此外，同步翻譯必須注意以下的高度技巧。

- ◉　**將長句濃縮**

- ◉　**細部省略，譯出重點**

- ◉　**能夠預見話題的發展，以免偏離。**

例如以下的這段話：「我想在洛杉磯舉行貿易商展。你們以為如何？」，一般可能譯成：

"I have been thinking of holding a trade fair in Los Angeles. What do you think？"

但是同時翻譯時，不能一口氣聽完再譯，所以會有所差別。請見以下的譯法：

「我　想　在　　洛　杉　磯　　　　舉　行　貿　易　商　展，
　　　　　　　Los Angeles　‥‥　　　　Trade Fair

你　　們　　以　　爲　　如　　何　？
is what I have in mind.‥‥‥　How about this?」

必須如此這般地，暫停……，整理調整……，快速譯出，所以難免和原文有些許差距。又因爲是零零碎碎拼湊起來的，如果無法預測下文，可能連肯定、否定都譯反。因此，這種預測的工夫絕不可少。

下面請看英譯中的情況：

"I have no objection, if you think we can get a big
　我　不　反　對，　如果你們認爲　　‥‥‥‥‥
enough number of food companies interested.
　許　多　食　品　公　司　感　興　趣　。"

由上可知，這種翻譯總是會有點不合乎原有的中文說法。本來……部分不必譯出，但是可以一邊慢慢譯，一邊構思下面的句子，以便減少停頓不順暢的感覺。

同時，翻譯也需要一段時間磨練，可自行利用錄音帶試著做練習，才能有長足的進步。

② 秘書翻譯自我測驗

【情況】：陳副董事長的客戶韓特先生，未曾事先定下約會就貿然來訪，但是陳副董不在辦公室，而韓特必須找一位主管商討更改契約的事。

於是秘書趙莉莉小姐就帶他去見江總務主任，而江先生要求趙小姐翻譯，於是她就充當了 ad hoc interpreter（特別翻譯）。

你若是趙小姐，會怎樣翻譯下面的話呢？

Hunt : I'm sorry to trouble you about this, but my home office insists that it be settled before the contract is signed.

Chao : (1) _____

Chiang : 預備什麼時候訂契約？

Chao : (2) _____

Hunt : Three days from now.

Chao : (3) _____

Chiang : 我懂了，那麼，你們公司想變更什麼？

Chao : (4) _____

Hunt : It concerns the representation our side would have if a disagreement arose in the future.

Chao : I'm sorry, but I don't understand exactly what you mean by "representation."

Hunt : Oh, sorry. What I mean is that we don't know if our lawyer can represent us here in Taiwan. It's a legal question. If some problem arises, we would want to use our own lawyer.

Chao : (5) _____

Chiang : 是這樣的，這是個相當專門的問題，但是以前合夥時就發生了同樣的問題，我會請公司的法律專家核查細節，並作成報告給您。

Chao : (6) _____

Hunt : How soon can I have it?

Chao : (7) _____

Chiang : 我馬上叫人準備並譯成英文，您明天來拿好嗎？

Chao : (8) _____

Hunt : Yes, thank you, that would be fine. Then I'll inform the home office immediately.

Chao : (9) _____

解　答

(1) 對不起要麻煩您，但是我們公司堅持在訂契約之前，解決這一點。

(2) When is the contract to be signed?

(3) 三天後。

(4) I see. What is the change your office wants to make?

(5) 是法律問題，如果將來發生什麼糾紛，我們想用自己的律師做代理人。

(6) I see. That's quite a technical question, but it has come up before in previous joint-venture contracts. Mr. Chiang will have our expert on legal matters check the details and prepare a statement for you.

(7) 我什麼時候可以拿到?

(8) Mr. Chiang will have someone prepare it right away and translate it into English. Could you come back tomorrow and pick it up?

(9) 好的,謝謝。我立刻向公司報告。

(3)　I see. Then　（ollor ）… In later speech in但 it it the
sure in the image the cause the source while the time for to by
by the entry Chang, withdraw and After,… or beat inner of of
their the serials and mer agree　離 anoncer for in to
mar, itra, all it to.

(4) New man, with the a you to a person it man a of
in to entire to by in English. is able or your self
ever-ma. All it will to a commanding or a commanding an
at more next, on.

第7章

秘書電話英語

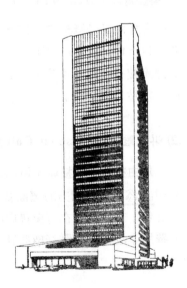

⭐⭐⭐ 1) 打國際電話的方法 ⭐⭐⭐

對任何公司的新進職員來說，電話英語大概是最令人煩惱的吧！平常接到本國人的電話尚不知如何應付，更何況是和外國人通話。平常口頭英語尚可稍賴表情以猜測其意，打電話則完全看不見對方，祇能依靠自己的耳朵和平素的聽力訓練。最近，打國際電話的趨向越來越明顯，在與國外有交易的公司工作，確實有必要瞭解電話英語的基本常識，以及各種情況並加以演練，以期趁早摸熟其訣竅，增進自己的工作實力。（本公司出版有「電話英語」專書，讀者可參考）

以下針對秘書電話英語須知的各種基本常識，分別敍述，並依情況分類，各舉實例示範。

(1) 叫號電話（Station Call）

這種電話是祇指定對方號碼的電話。可向接線生指定電話號碼，並告之以 Station Call 即可，和國內長途電話一樣，從對方接話起計費，是透過接線生電話中最便宜的一種。但若是你要找的人不在，他人接話時也需按時間計費。

(2) 叫人電話（Personal Call）

是由接線生叫接你想通話的人；首先你必須告訴接線生是 Personal Call，然後再把對方的電話號碼和名字告訴他，當接線生幫你叫人時不予計費，若對方不在可免費取消這通電話，但若對方已接話，需加上叫人費用，故比叫號電話稍微貴一點。

(3) 對方付費電話（Collect Call）

這是由接話的一方付費的電話，首先，要告訴接線生是 Collect Call，再告知對方電話號碼及人名，然後由接線生叫出對方，得到對方承諾付費方予以接通。這對出國旅遊或出差的人打回家裏或公司來說，較爲方便。

(4) 信用卡電話（Credit Card Call）

首先必須申請發給國際電話用信用卡，才能使用。由於在申請時就已由公司或個人付過費，所以打電話時不需再用現金。這對經常出差的生意人是非常方便實惠的。

(5) 國際直撥電話

這是可以不透過接線生自行接通的電話，和使用國內電話的方式幾無不同，能夠以極快的速度和美國、歐洲、亞洲各大城市的對象通話。費用以 6 秒爲單位計費，比透過接線生的國際電話來得經濟。但是也必須先登記，方能自由使用。

2）秘書電話英語實例

用英語講電話時，請注意以下四點。

(i) *Speak clearly* （說清楚）

(ii) *Speak slowly* （說慢點）

(iii) *Don't hesitate to speak* （請直說）

(iv) *Write down the message* （請記錄要旨）

(1) 打電話

① 傳達自己姓名時⋯⋯⋯⋯⋯	This is *Mr. Wu speaking.*
（我是～。）	This is *Mr. Wu from Taipei.*
	This is *Mr. Wu of International Trading Co..*
② 叫出對方時⋯⋯⋯⋯⋯⋯⋯	May I $\begin{Bmatrix} \text{speak with} \\ \text{speak to} \end{Bmatrix}$ *Mr. Smith?*
（請～聽電話好嗎？）	I'd like to talk $\begin{Bmatrix} \text{with} \\ \text{to} \end{Bmatrix}$ *Mr. Smith.*
③ 詢問對方姓名時⋯⋯⋯⋯⋯	Who is this, please?
（您是那一位？）	Who is speaking, please?
	Who is calling, please?
	May I have your name, please?
	May I ask who is calling?
	* Is this Mr. Smith?
	（您是史密斯先生嗎？）
④ 當對方不在而必須詢問⋯⋯	When will he $\begin{Bmatrix} \text{be} \\ \text{come} \end{Bmatrix}$ back?
何時回來	
（他什麼時候會回來呢？）	When is he expected to be back?
	Can（Could）you tell me what time he'll be there?
	Do you know what time he will be in?

⑤ 要留話時⋯⋯⋯⋯⋯⋯⋯⋯Will you take a message?

（請轉達他～好嗎？）　Can I leave a message?

I'd like to leave a message.

（請轉達他回電話給我。）Will you tell him to call me back?

（請轉達他～先生打過電　Will you tell him that *Mr. Chao* is

話。）　　　　　　calling?

---

⑥ 打內線電話時⋯⋯⋯⋯⋯Ext. 345, please.

（請接內線～號。）　Will you connect me with 864?

Let me have Ext. 5977, please.

May I have Ext. 521?

I want Ext. 111.

Will you please give me 439?

---

⑦ 打到對方的部門，某人⋯⋯May I have *the Foreign Depart-*

辦公室時　　　　　*ment*?

（請接～部門。）　Will (Would, Could) you connect

me with *the Export Section*?

（請接～部門的～。）　I'd like to speak to *Mr. Adams,*

the manager of General Affairs.

Will (Would, Could) you call *Mr.*

Adams of the Import Section?

May I speak to anyone in charge

of the Sales Project?

(2) 接電話

① 本人來接電話時 ············· （我是～。）	Speaking. This is *Mr. Chen* speaking. This is $\begin{Bmatrix} he. \\ she. \end{Bmatrix}$
② 詢問對方有什麼事時 ········ （你有什麼事？）	May I help you? What can I do for you?
③ 請對方等待片刻時 ·········· （請稍待。）	One moment, please. Just a minute, please. Hold on, please. Hold the line, please.
④ 讓對方久等時 ················ （對不起讓你久等了。）	Thank you for waiting. I am sorry to keep you waiting. I'm sorry to have kept you waiting.
⑤ 詢問打給何人時 ·············· （您要找誰？）	Whom are you calling? Whom would you like to speak to?
⑥ 詢問打給哪一部門時 ········ （您找哪一部門？）	What section (department) are you calling? What section (department) is he in? What section shall I connect with?

⑦ 當有同姓兩人以上，詢 ······ We have two（three ···）*Andersons* .
問所屬部門（名字）時　　May I have his department（first
　　　　　　　　　　　　name)?

（我們有兩位同姓的人，　We have several persons by that
請告訴我他所屬的部門　　name. Do you know what depart-
（名字）好嗎？）　　　　ment he's in?

---

⑧ 本人不在而轉接其他部 ······ I'll switch（transfer）this call
門時　　　　　　　　　　to *Mr. Adams*（Ext. ～ , ～ sec-
　　　　　　　　　　　　tion).

（我把這通電話轉給～。）I'll connect you with *the depart-
　　　　　　　　　　　　ment in charge*.

　　　　　　　　　　　　We'll give you *the manager of
　　　　　　　　　　　　General Affairs*.

---

⑨ 本人不在或其他情況 ········ He is out now.
（他不在。他出去了。）He is not in now.
　　　　　　　　　　　　He is not at home.
　　　　　　　　　　　　He is not available right now.
　　　　　　　　　　　　He has just stepped out now.
　　　　　　　　　　　　He is out of town.

（他正在接電話。）　　He is talking on another line.
（他已經調到～了。）　He has been transferred to *the
　　　　　　　　　　　　Taipei office*.

　　　　　　　　　　　　He is now at *the Taipei office*.

（他到～出差去了。）　He is on a business trip to *Hong
　　　　　　　　　　　　Kong* now.

	He left for *Hong Kong* on business yesterday.
（他今天請假。）	He is not working today.
	He is off today.
	He is absent today.
（他在開會。）	He is attending a meeting.
	He is at a meeting now.
	He is in conference.

⑩ 請對方留話時……………	May I take a message?
（您要留話嗎？）	Would you like to leave a message?

⑪ 對方打錯電話時…………	You have the wrong number.
（你撥錯電話號碼了。）	

(3) 其他

① 聽不清楚時…………………	Pardon me.
（我聽不清楚，請再說一 次。）	I beg your pardon?
	I can't hear you very well.
	I can hardly hear you.
	Will you repeat it again?
	Will you speak a little louder?
	Will you speak more slowly?
	*Can you hear me all right?
	（你聽得清楚嗎？）

② 電話中 ························· The line is busy.
（他正在用電話。）　　The number is busy.

③ 沒有人接話時 ··············· The number doesn't answer.
（沒有回答）　　　　 Nobody answers.
　　　　　　　　　　　There is no reply.

④ 電話故障時 ················· The telephone is out of order.
（電話壞了。）

⑤ 請求掛斷時 ················· Hang up, please.
（請掛斷電話。）

⑥ 接到我方付費國 ··········· Will you accept the charges?
　際電話時　　　　　　Will you pay for the call?
（你願意付費嗎？）　*Yes, I will（accept them）.
—國外接線生　　　　Please tell me the time and
　　　　　　　　　　　charges.
（請告訴我時間和費用。）Will you let me know the time
　　　　　　　　　　　and charges?

⑦ 時間的説法
　　　　　 8:00 AM······（around）eight o'clock in the
　　　　　　　　　　　morning
　　　　　 9:15 AM······ a quarter past nine in the morn-
　　　　　　　　　　　ing
　　　　　 3:30 PM······ three thirty in the afternoon

6:55 PM‥‥‥ five minutes to seven in the evening

30 分鐘後‥‥‥ in thirty minutes（in half an
hour）

一小時半後‥‥‥ in one hour and a half

2 小時後‥‥‥ in two hours

兩、三天後‥‥‥ in a few days

＊What time is it now?

（現在幾點？）

⑧ **數字的説法** ‥‥‥‥‥‥‥‥‥ Telephone number 202-5611

（two $\left\{ \begin{matrix} oh \\ zero \end{matrix} \right\}$ two five six one
one）

Room number 425（four twenty
five）

Extension number 3160

（three one six $\begin{matrix} oh \\ zero \end{matrix}$ ）

【 秘書電話須知 】

① 善用 this

電話交談和面對面會話不同，所以都不用 I am（我是…）或
You are（你是～），而用抽象名詞 This is（這兒是～）。同樣
地，詢問「您是誰？」時，不宜用 Who are you? 這是不禮貌的，
應該用較爲客氣的 Who is this speaking?

② 注意時差問題

當我們打電話給國外客戶，而對方說「他不在，請於明天×點打來。」時，你得換算我方打電話的時間，別莽莽撞撞地照本地時間打電話過去，搞不好正是三更半夜，氣得對方都不想跟你打交道。這固然太誇張了，但也確實是電話禮儀，不得不小心。

❊ 秘書電話英語實況會話

以下引用英文電話應對實例，做為具體的參考。

(1) 對方立即接電話時

實　例

Foreign Party :	Hello.
Mr. Wu :	Hello. This is Mr. Wu from Taipei, Taiwan. May I speak to Mr. Anderson, Please?
Foreign Party :	One moment, please. ·········
Mr. Anderson :	This is Mr. Anderson speaking.

外國方面：喂。

　　吳先生：喂。我是台灣台北的吳先生。請安得森先生聽電話。

外國方面：請稍待。·········

　　安得森：我是安得森。

(2) 對方不在時

```
┌──────────────── 實　例 ────────────────┐

    Mrs. Wu : Hello. This is Taiwan calling. Is Miss
              Julia Chao there?
Foreign Party : Hold the line, please. I will check.
              ········· I am sorry to have kept you
              waiting. She hasn't come back yet.
              But she should be here soon. Would
              you like to call again later?
    Mrs. Wu : All right, I will do that.
              Thank you. Good bye.

└──────────────────────────────────────┘
```

吳太太　　：喂，這是台灣打來的電話。請問趙茱莉小姐在不在？

外國方面：請不要掛斷，我看看………對不起讓您久等。她還沒
　　　　　回來，但是她應該馬上就會回來。您待會兒再打來好
　　　　　嗎？

吳太太　　：好的，謝謝，再見。

(3) 對方不在須留話

```
┌──────────────── 實　例 ────────────────┐

Foreign Party : Hello.
    Mr. Wu : Hello. May I speak to Mr. J.C. Miller,
              please?

└──────────────────────────────────────┘
```

Foreign Party : I'm sorry, he is out now. Who's call-
　　　　　　　ing, please?

Mr. Wu : This is Mr. Wu from Taipei calling.
　　　　　　When will he be back?

Foreign Party : He won't be back until late tonight.
　　　　　　　May I take a message?

Mr. Wu : Yes, will you tell him to call me back
　　　　　as soon as he comes in? I will give
　　　　　you my telephone number in Taipei. It
　　　　　is（02）7086554.

Foreign Party : All right, Mr. Wu, I will give him
　　　　　　　your message.

Mr. Wu : Thank you. Good-bye.

外國方面：喂。

吳先生　：喂，請 J.C. 米勒先生聽電話好嗎?

外國方面：對不起，他現在不在。請問您哪裏找?

吳先生　：我是台北的吳先生。他什麼時候回來?

外國方面：他今晚很遲才會回來，您留個話好嗎?

吳先生　：好的，請您轉告他回來立刻回我電話。我台北的電話
　　　　　號碼是（02）7086554。

外國方面：好的，吳先生。我會告訴他。

吳先生　：謝謝，再見。

⑷ 打到旅館請客戶接電話

實　例

Hotel operator : Century Hotel. May I help you?

Mrs. Wu : May I speak to Mr. Billy Chao?

Hotel operator : Do you know his room number?

Mrs. Wu : I'm sorry, I don't.

Hotel operator : Will you spell his name, please?

Mrs. Wu : Yes, the first name is Billy, B—I—
L—L—Y, and the last name is Chao,
C—H—A—O.

Hotel operator : Thank you. One moment, please. ………
His room number is 722 and he is on
the line. Go ahead, please.

旅館接線生：世紀飯店，請問有什麼事？

吳　太　太：請趙比利先生聽電話好嗎？

旅館接線生：您知道他的房間號碼嗎？

吳　太　太：對不起，我不知道。

旅館接線生：請您拼出他的名字。

吳　太　太：好的，名字是比利，B—I—L—L—Y，姓是趙，
C—H—A—O。

旅館接線生：謝謝你，請稍待。………他的房間號碼是722，他
已接了電話，請說吧。

(5) 上司不在時接電話

```
━━━━━━━━━━━━  實  例  ━━━━━━━━━━━━

Hong Kong operator :   Hello. This is Hong Kong calling.
                       We have an overseas call for Mr.
                       Wu. May I speak to him?

     Taipei Party ::   I'm sorry, he is on a business
                       trip to New York now.

Hong Kong operator :   Do you know the telephone num-
                       ber in New York?

     Taipei Party :    Yes, just a moment, please.……
                       … Thank you for waiting. The
                       number in New York is（06）
                       240-4111, Ext. 356.

Hong Kong operator :   I see. Thank you very much.
                       Good-bye.

     Taipei Party :    You're welcome. Good-bye.
```

香港接線生：喂，這兒是香港，有一通吳先生的越洋電話。請他
　　　　　　聽電話好嗎？

台北方面　：對不起，他現在到紐約出差去了。

香港接線生：你知道紐約的電話號碼嗎？

台北方面　：知道，請稍待。………讓您久等了，紐約的電話號
　　　　　　碼是（06）240-4111, 轉356。

香港接線生：我知道了，多謝。再見。

台北方面　：不客氣。再見。

⑹ 從國外打電話回台灣

――――――――― 實 例 ―――――――――

Operator : Overseas operator. May I help you?

Mr. Wu : Yes, operator, I'd like to place a collect
call to Taiwan.

Operator : What number are you calling?

Mr. Wu : I'm calling Taipei. The number is（02）708-
6554.

Operator : Whom would you like to talk to, sir?

Mr. Wu : I'd like to talk to Mrs. Wu.

Operator : May I have your name and telephone number,
please?

Mr. Wu : I'm calling from the Hawaii Hilton Hotel.
The number is 735-1000, Room 711. My
name is Ta-hwa Wu.

Operator : All right, sir. If you hang up, we'll call
you back in a minute.

Mr. Wu : Thank you, operator.

Operator : You're welcome.

接線生：國外接線生，有什麼事嗎？

吳先生：是的，我想打一通對方付費的電話到台灣。

接線生：您打幾號？

吳先生：我打到台北，電話號碼是（02）7086554。

接線生：您要和誰說話？

吳先生：我想打給吳太太。

接線生：請告訴我您的姓名和電話號碼，好嗎？

吳先生：我是在夏威夷希爾頓飯店打的電話，號碼是735-1000，711號房，我是吳大華。

接線生：好的，先生。請您先掛斷電話，我待會兒會打過來。

吳先生：謝謝。

接線生：不客氣。

(7) 接國外電話

實　例

Honolulu operator : This is Honolulu. We have a collect call for Mrs. Wu from Mr. Wu. May I speak to her ?

Mrs. Wu : This is Mrs. Wu.

Honolulu operator : Will you accept the charges?

Mrs. Wu : Yes, I will.

Honolulu operator : Thank you, ma'am. Mr. Wu, your party is on the line. Go ahead, please.

檀香山接線生：這兒是檀香山。吳先生打對方付費電話給吳太太請她聽電話好嗎？

吳　太　太　：我是吳太太。

檀香山接線生：您願意付費嗎？

吳　太　太　：是的 。

檀香山接線生：謝謝您 ，夫人 。吳先生 ，對方已接了電話 ，請說
　　　　　　　吧 。

(8) 對方直接對話

> **實　例**
>
> *Mr. Chiang* : This is Mr. Chiang from Taipei. May I
> speak to Mrs. Jones?
> *Mrs. Jones* : Speaking.

江先生　　：我是台北的江先生 。請瓊斯太太聽電話 ，好嗎？
瓊斯太太：我就是 。

(9) 對方由接線生接話

> **實　例**
>
> *Office Operator* : Empire Incorporated. May I help you?
> *Mr. Wu* : May I speak to Mr. Adams in the
> Export Section?
> *Office Operator* : May I have your name, please?
> *Mr. Wu* : This is Mr. Wu of International
> Trading Company, Taiwan.
> *Office Operator* : Just a moment, please. ·········Mr.
> Adams is on the line. Go ahead, please.

辦公室接線生：帝國股份有限公司，請問有什麼事？

吳　先　生　：請出口部的亞當斯先生聽電話好嗎？

辦公室接線生：請問您是哪一位？

吳　先　生　：我是台灣國際貿易公司的吳先生。

辦公室接線生：請稍待。………亞當斯先生已接了電話，請說吧。

⑽ 指定內線電話無人接話時

實　例

> *Mr. Wu* : Is this Empire Incorporated?
>
> *Office Operator* : Yes, it is. May I help you?
>
> *Mr. Wu* : Ext. 453, please.
>
> *Office Operator* : 453?
>
> *Mr. Wu* : Yes.
>
> *Office Operator* : Thank you. One moment, please. ……
> … I'm sorry, but nobody answers
> right now.
>
> *Mr. Wu* : I see …… Well ……
>
> *Office Operator* : What section are you calling?
>
> *Mr. Wu* : I'm calling the Textile Department.
>
> *Office Operator* : Whom are you calling in the Textile
> Department?
>
> *Mr. Wu* : I'm calling Mr. Adams.
>
> *Office Operator* : We'll check the number. One moment,
> please.

Mr. Wu : Thank you.

Office Operator : You're welcome. ………

Hello, sir. The correct number for
Mr. Adams is 543.

Mr. Wu : Oh, 543?

Office Operator : Yes, we'll put you through.

Just a moment, please.

Mr. Wu : Thank you.

Office Operator : You're welcome. ………

Mr. Adams is on the line now.

Go ahead, please.

吳　先　生 ：是帝國股份有限公司嗎？
辦公室接線生：是的，請問有什麼事？

吳　先　生 ：請接內線453。
辦公室接線生：453嗎？

吳　先　生 ：是的。
辦公室接線生：謝謝您，請等一下。………對不起，現在沒人接。

吳　先　生 ：我知道了。……… 嗯……
辦公室接線生：您要打到哪個部門？

吳　先　生 ：我打織品部。
辦公室接線生：您打給織品部的哪一位？

吳　先　生 ：我找亞當斯先生。
辦公室接線生：我查一下電話號碼。請稍等。

吳　先　生　：謝謝。

辦公室接線生：不客氣。………喂，亞當斯先生處的正確號碼是
543 號。

吳　先　生　：是 543 嗎？

辦公室接線生：是的，我幫您接通。請稍待。

吳　先　生　：謝謝。

辦公室接線生：不客氣。………亞當斯先生已接電話，請說。

⑾ 有數位同姓者在場

實　例

Mr. Wu : Mr. Smith, please.

Office Operator : We have many Smiths.

May I have his first name or his section?

Mr. Wu : I don't know his section, but his first initial is K.

Office Operator : I see. Just a moment, please. ………

We're trying to locate him.

Hold the line, please.

Mr. Wu : All right.

Office Operator : I'm sorry to have kept you waiting.

He is coming to the phone now.

Mr. Wu : Thank you.

Office Operator : Now, Mr. Smith is on the line.

Go ahead, please.

吳　先　生　：請史密斯先生聽電話。

辦公室接線生：我們這兒有好多位史密斯。請告訴我他的名字或部門好嗎？

吳　先　生　：我不知道他的部門，但他的名字第一個字母是K。

辦公室接線生：我知道了，請稍等。………我們試著找找看。請別掛斷。

吳　先　生　：好的。

辦公室接線生：對不起讓您久等了。他要來接電話了。

吳　先　生　：謝謝。

辦公室接線生：現在他接電話了，請說吧。

(12) 對方不在時

實　例

Foreign Party : This is Atlantic Company.

　　　　　　　　May I help you?

　　Mr. Wu : May I speak to Mr. Taylor of the Iron & Steel Department?

Foreign Party : Mr. Taylor? One moment, please. ………

　　　　　　　　I'm sorry he's not in now.

　　　　　　　　He'll be back in 30 minutes.

　　Mr. Wu : Thank you.

　　　　　　　　I'll call him later.

外國方面：大西洋公司，請問有什麼事？

吳先生　：請鋼鐵部的泰勒先生聽電話好嗎？

外國方面：泰勒先生嗎？請等一下，………對不起，他現在不在。
他會在30分鐘之內回來。

吳先生　　：謝謝您，我待會兒再打來。

秘書必備常識

Identification Marks 是什麼？

信的左下角打上的識別記號，表示這封信的執筆者與謄打者，以確定其責任。記號是各探執筆者（Writer）和打字員（Typist）名字的第一個字母構成。例如，執筆者是 Billy Chao，打字員是 Lilly Wu 時，其署名就是 BC：lw 或 BC／lw。

⒀ 對方不在，有人代理接話時

實　例

Mr. Wu : May I speak to Mr. White of the Machinery Section?

Foreign Party : Mr. White?

Mr. Wu : Yes, he is the chief of the section.

Foreign Party : Thank you.

One moment, please. ………

I'm sorry, but he's not available right now.

Do you want to speak to anyone else?

> *Mr. Wu* : Let me see.
>
> How about Mr. Roberts?
>
> *Foreign Party* : One moment, please. ………
>
> Mr. Roberts is on the line.

吳先生　　：請機械科的懷特先生聽電話好嗎？

外國方面：懷特先生嗎？

吳先生　　：是的，他是該科的科長。

外國方面：謝謝。請等一下。………對不起，他現在不能接電話。

您要和別人說話嗎？

吳先生　　：我想想看。羅勃玆先生可以嗎？

外國方面：請稍等。………他接電話了。

⒁ 對方正在開會

實　例

> *Mr. Wu* : Let me speak to Mr. Williams, please.
>
> *Foreign Party* : I'm sorry, but he is at a meeting now.
>
> *Mr. Wu* : When will it be finished?
>
> *Foreign Party* : It will be finished around four o'clock.
>
> *Mr. Wu* : I see. I'll call him around four o'clock
> your time.
>
> *Foreign Party* : Thank you.
>
> I'll give him the message.

吳先生　：請威廉斯先生聽電話。

外國方面：對不起，他現在正在開會。

吳先生　：什麼時候結束呢？

外國方面：四點左右會結束。

吳先生：：我知道了，我會在貴地時間四點左右再打來。

外國方面：謝謝，我會轉告他。

⒂ 詢問對方去處

實 例

> *Mr. Wu* : Mr. Richards, please.
>
> *Foreign Party* : Mr. Richards?
>
> He is out of San Francisco.
>
> *Mr. Wu* : Oh, he isn't in San Francisco.
>
> Where can I reach him?
>
> *Foreign Party* : He is in Los Angeles.
>
> I'll give you his telephone number
> there.
>
> Just a minute, please. ………
>
> The number is（213）211-4321.
>
> *Mr. Wu* : Los Angeles（213）211-4321?
>
> *Foreign Party* : That's right.
>
> *Mr. Wu* : I'll call him there.
>
> Thank you.
>
> *Foreign Party* : You're welcome.

吳先生　　：請李察斯先生聽電話。

外國方面：李察斯先生嗎？他不在舊金山。

吳先生　　：哦！他不在舊金山，那麼他在哪兒呢？

外國方面：他在洛杉磯。我告訴您他那裏的電話號碼。請等一下。
　　　　　………電話是（213）211-4321。

吳先生　　：洛杉磯（213）211-4321？

外國方面：是的。

吳先生　　：我會打到那兒找他。謝謝您。

外國方面：不客氣。

⒃ 接受對方付費電話時

實　例

American Operator :　This is the United States Operator.
　　　　　　　　　　　Is this Taipei（02）3319948?

Taipei Party :　Yes, it is.
　　　　　　　　May I help you?

American Operator :　We have a collect call for Mr. Chen
　　　　　　　　　　　from Mr. Fitzgerald.

Taipei Party :　A collect call for Mr. Chen from
　　　　　　　　Mr. Fitzgerald.
　　　　　　　　May I have his department?

American Operator :　The Non-Ferrous Metals Department.

Taipei Party :　Just a moment, please. ………
　　　　　　　　We'll accept the charges.
　　　　　　　　Will you let us know the time and
　　　　　　　　charges after the call?

American Operator：　Yes, I will.

　　　Taipei Party：　Thank you.

　　　　　　　　　　Mr. Chen is on the line.

　　　　　　　　　　Go ahead, please.

美國接線生：這是美國接線生。這兒是（02）3319948 嗎？

台北方面　：是的。有什麼可以幫忙的？

美國接線生：有一通費滋傑羅先生打給貴處陳先生的付費電話。

台北方面　：是費滋傑羅先生打給陳先生，我方付費的電話，我
　　　　　　可以知道他是什麼部門的嗎？

美國接線生：非鐵金屬部門。

台北方面　：請等一下。………我方付費。通話結束後請告訴我
　　　　　　時間及費用。

美國接線生：好的。

台北方面　：謝謝，陳先生已接電話，請說。

【 秘書電話須知 】

　　萬一你撥錯了電話，該怎麼說好呢？最好是客氣地說聲 I
am sorry. 或 I dialed incorrectly. 表示歉意。

★★★ 3) 電話中傳達名字拼法 ★★★

　　無論是國人唸外國人名字，或是外國人唸國人的名字時，都會感到
特別不習慣。因此，下面列出在電話中告知對方自己的姓名時，應把握
的要領。

◎ My name is Julia, J for Japan, U for Union, L for London, I for Italy, A for America. 以下是26個字母的 Spelling Analogy Code。

A	America	J	Japan	S	Spain
B	Bombay	K	King	T	Tokyo
C	China	L	London	U	Union
D	Denmark	M	Mexico	V	Victory
E	England	N	New York	W	Washington
F	France	O	Oslo	X	X-ray
G	Germany	P	Peking	Y	Year
H	Hong Kong	Q	Queen	Z	Zebra
I	Italy	R	Rome		

第8章

國際禮儀電報

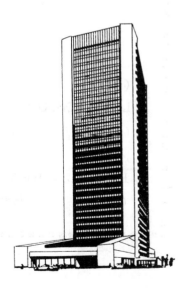

國際禮儀電報的擬定

通訊業已進入新媒體的今天，電傳打字（Telex）的使用也隨之普遍起來。但是，如果弔唁函電、祝賀函電、也使用縮寫的電傳打字，恐怕太過失禮。有必要正正式式地擬一封電報。

禮儀電報除了漂亮的電報用紙和漂亮的信封包裝起來之外，最好不要使用太多的簡字、略語，以下所列者為國際禮儀電報的典型電文。讀者可應情況需要選其中適合的來使用。

禮儀電報

使用方法：在收文人名之前需加註"祝賀"或"弔唁"之
意旨。

（例）
LX＝ABCDCO SEOUL
（祝賀）　　　　　（抬頭）

LXDEUIL＝JOHN LEE C/O XYZINC HAMBURG
（弔唁）　　　　　（抬頭）

1）祝賀客戶或同業結婚（MARRIAGE）

1. CONGRATULATIONS ON YOUR HAPPY WEDDING
2. CONGRATULATIONS AND LASTING HAPPINESS
   TO YOU BOTH
3. CONGRATULATIONS AND MY（OUR）BEST
   WISHES FOR MANY YEARS OF HAPPINESS
4. MAY YOU HAVE MANY HAPPY RETURNS OF
   WEDDING ANNIVERSARIES
5. HEARTIEST CONGRATULATIONS I WISH YOU
   MANY YEARS OF HAPPINESS
6. CONGRATULATIONS AND MY（OUR）VERY
   BEST WISHES TO A HAPPY COUPLE
7. CONGRATULATIONS ON YOUR WEDDING AND
   BEST WISHES FOR YOUR FUTURE HAPPINESS
8. TO THE BRIDE AND GROOM LOVE AND CON-
   GRATULATIONS FROM AN OLD FRIEND
9. WE ALL JOIN IN HEARTY CONGRATULATIONS
   AND BEST WISHES FOR YOUR HAPPINESS
10. MAY HAPPINESS HEALTH AND PROSPERITY BE
    WITH YOU THROUGH THE YEARS TO COME
11. HEARTIEST CONGRATULATIONS ON YOUR
    MARRIAGE AND BEST WISHES FOR MANY
    YEARS TO COME

12. SINCERE CONGRATULATIONS ON YOUR SONS
　　（DAUGHTERS）WEDDING PLEASE CONVEY
　　MY（OUR）VERY BEST WISHES FOR EVERY
　　HAPPINESS IN THEIR NEW LIFE

13. HEARTY CONGRATULATIONS ON YOUR MAR-
　　RIAGE MAY MUCH HAPPINESS BE BROUGHT
　　TO YOU AND YOUR LOVELY WIFE FOR MANY
　　YEARS TO COME

1. 恭賀新婚愉快。

2. 恭賀新婚並願兩位永遠快樂。

3. 恭賀二位並祝福永遠快樂。

4. 願永遠有快樂的結婚紀念日。

5. 誠摯地祝福你們永遠快樂。

6. 恭喜，並衷心祝福這對快樂的佳偶。

7. 恭喜新婚，祝你們未來幸福。

8. 老友祝新郎新娘永浴愛河。

9. 全體祝賀兩位，並願永遠快樂。

10. 願快樂、健康、幸運永遠與你們同在。

11. 恭賀新婚，並祝永遠快樂。

12. 恭賀令郎（令媛）新婚，並祝新生活充滿快樂。

13. 衷心恭賀新婚，願你和新娘永遠快樂。

◆　　　　　◆　　　　　◆

【註】　prosperity〔prɑs′pɛrətɪ〕*n*. 成功；幸運；繁榮

　　　convey〔kən′ve〕*n*. 轉達；通報

2) 祝賀客戶或同業弄璋（瓦）之喜

（BIRTH）

實 例

1. CONGRATULATIONS ON （THE） BIRTH OF YOUR SON （DAUGHTER, CHILD）

2. LOVE TO THE DEAR MOTHER AND HER LITTLE SON （DAUGHTER）

3. HEARTY CONGRATULATIONS ON THE ARRIVAL OF THE NEW SON （DAUGHTER）

4. WE ARE ALL DELIGHTED TO HEAR THE NEWS HEARTY CONGRATULATIONS

5. BEST WISHES TO THE NEWLY ARRIVED SON （DAUGHTER） AND TO HIS （HER） MOTHER

6. A WARM WELCOME TO THE NEW ARRIVAL AND BEST WISHES FOR HIS （HER） HEALTH AND HAPPINESS

7. VERY PLEASED TO HEAR YOU HAVE A FINE YOUNG SON MY SINCERE WISHES TO HIM FOR A LONG AND HAPPY LIFE

1. 恭喜令郎（令嬡、小孩）的誕生。
2. 對母親及小兒子（女兒）表示我的愛。
3. 衷心地祝賀令郎（令嬡）的誕生。

4. 我們都很高興聽說您平安生產，並獻上衷心的祝福。

5. 問候新生兒（女）與他（她）的母親。

6. 由衷恭賀新生兒的誕生並願（她）健康、幸福。

7. 聽說你生了個健康寶寶，眞是萬分高興，並祝福他有綿長、幸福的一生。

3）祝賀客戶或同業生日（BIRTHDAY）

實　例

1. HAPPY BIRTHDAY （TO YOU）
2. CONGRATULATIONS ON THIS HAPPY DAY
3. CONGRATULATIONS ON YOUR 50TH BIRTHDAY
4. BEST WISHES FOR A HAPPY BIRTHDAY
5. （ALL OF US WISH YOU）MANY HAPPY RE-TURNS OF THE DAY
6. HEARTY CONGRATULATIONS ON YOUR BIRTH-DAY AND WISHING YOU GOOD HEALTH
7. MY BEST WISHES ARE WITH YOU ON YOUR BIRTHDAY
8. BEST WISHES FOR YOUR BIRTHDAY MAY YOU LIVE LONG AND PROSPEROUSLY
9. MY AFFECTIONATE THOUGHTS AND EVERY GOOD WISH TO YOU ON YOUR BIRTHDAY
10. I WISH I COULD BE WITH YOU TODAY BEST WISHES FOR A HAPPY BIRTHDAY

11. CONGRATULATIONS ON YOUR 60TH ANNIVER-
    SARY AND MY VERY BEST WISHES FOR MANY
    YEARS OF HEALTH AND HAPPINESS
12. THE BEST OF ALL GOOD THINGS FOR THIS
    BIRTHDAY AND ALL THE MANY MORE TO
    COME
13. WE ALL JOIN IN WISHING YOU A VERY HAPPY
    BIRTHDAY AND MANY YEARS OF HEALTH
    AND PROSPERITY

1. 祝(您)生日快樂。
2. 祝賀這快樂的日子。
3. 恭賀五十壽辰。
4. 祈願生日快樂。
5. （同賀）年年生日快樂。
6. 由衷祝賀生日愉快、身體健康。
7. 我由衷的祝福與您的生日同在。
8. 恭賀誕辰，願您長壽幸福。
9. 用我的情意與祝福恭賀您的生日。
10. 可惜不能與您共度生日，祝福您生日快樂。
11. 恭賀六十大壽，並祝永遠健康、快樂。
12. 祝生日一切美好，祈願有更多的幸福降臨於你。
13. 同賀生日快樂，永遠健康、成功。

4） 祝賀晉昇、獲勝、開幕
（ **PROMOTION AND SUCCESS** ）

▨▨▨▨▨▨▨▨▨▨▨▨▨▨▨▨ 實 例 ▨▨▨▨▨▨▨▨▨▨▨▨▨▨▨▨

1. CONGRATULATIONS ON YOUR PROMOTION
   （ OPENING OF BUSINESS ）
2. DELIGHTED TO HEAR ABOUT YOUR PROMOTION
3. HEARTIEST CONGRATULATIONS ON YOUR
   SPLENDID VICTORY
4. SINCEREST CONGRATULATIONS ON YOUR
   SPLENDID SUCCESS
5. VERY PLEASED TO HEAR OF YOUR PROMOTION
6. YOU DESERVE THIS SPLENDID SUCCESS SIN-
   CEREST CONGRATULATIONS
7. SINCERE CONGRATULATIONS ON YOUR PROMO-
   TION （ TO THE RANK OF VICE-PRESIDENT ）
   AND BEST WISHES FOR YOUR FURTHER SUC-
   CESS
8. CONGRATULATIONS ON YOUR APPOINTMENT TO
   PRESIDENT AND SINCERE BEST WISHES FOR
   EVERY SUCCESS AND HAPPINESS （ IN YOUR
   NEW WORK ）

9. WE HAVE JUST HEARD OF YOUR SUCCESS
   SINCEREST CONGRATULATIONS AND BEST
   WISHES FOR THE FUTURE

10. CONGRATULATIONS TO YOU AND EVERY GOOD
    WISH FOR YOUR SUCCESS AND HAPPINESS IN
    YOUR NEW POSITION

11. CONGRATULATIONS ON YOUR APPOINTMENT
    AS MANAGER （I）WISH YOU GREAT SUC-
    CESS IN YOUR NEW POSITION AND HOPE
    OUR MUTUAL RELATIONSHIP WILL BE
    STRENGTHENED FURTHER

1. 恭賀昇遷（開業）。
2. 非常高興聽到您的昇遷。
3. 由衷祝賀您獲得輝煌的勝利。
4. 由衷恭賀您輝煌的勝利。
5. 非常高興聽到您昇遷。
6. 您輝煌的勝利實至名歸，謹表由衷祝賀之意。
7. 由衷祝賀昇遷（至副董的職位），並祈願您更加成功。
8. 恭賀您就任董事長，謹祝今後（在新職內）成功、快樂。
9. 剛接獲您成功的消息，衷心祝賀之餘，祈願今後更加飛黃騰達。
10. 恭喜，恭喜！願您就任新職後成功、如意。
11. 恭喜您就任經理之職，祈願您在新職位上一切順利，並希望更加強
    我們之間的關係。

【註】 promotion〔prə'moʃən〕*n.* 晉陞；昇遷　mutual〔'mjutʃυəl〕*adj* 相互的

5) 祝客戶或同業耶誕快樂
(CHRISTMAS GREETINGS)

實 例

1. SINCEREST SEASON GREETINGS
2. A MERRY CHRISTMAS AND A HAPPY NEW YEAR
3. BEST WISHES FOR CHRISTMAS AND A NEW YEAR
   (FILLED WITH SUCCESS AND HAPPINESS)
4. MAY CHRISTMAS BRING YOU JOY AND HAPPI-
   NESS
5. EVERY GOOD WISH FOR A MERRY CHRISTMAS
   AND A HAPPY NEW YEAR
6. WITH EVERY GOOD WISH FOR A MERRY CHRIST-
   MAS AND A HAPPY NEW YEAR
7. MAY PEACE JOY AND HAPPINESS BE WITH YOU
   FOR THIS HOLIDAY SEASON
8. WISHING YOU A BLESSED CHRISTMAS AND A
   NEW YEAR FILLED WITH HAPPINESS
9. ALL AFFECTION AND GOOD WISHES FOR A
   MERRY CHRISTMAS TO YOU AND YOURS
10. MAY THIS GREETING DO ITS SHARE TOWARD
    MAKING YOUR CHRISTMAS A PLEASANT ONE
11. A VERY MERRY CHRISTMAS AND ALL THE
    BEST WISHES FOR A HAPPY NEW YEAR

12. LOVE AND BEST WISHES FOR A MERRY
　　CHRISTMAS AND A HAPPY AND PROSPEROUS
　　NEW YEAR

13. MAY THE PEACE AND JOY OF THE CHRISTMAS
　　BE YOURS TODAY AND EVERY DAY
　　THROUGHOUT NEW YEAR

14. WISHING YOU ALL THE HAPPINESS OF THE
　　HOLIDAY SEASON AND THE BEST OF EVERY-
　　THING IN THE NEW YEAR

15. WITH THESE CHRISTMAS GREETINGS COME
　　SPECIAL THOUGHTS OF YOU AND WISHES
　　FOR YOUR HAPPINESS TODAY AND ALL YEAR
　　THROUGH

16. MAY THIS TELEGRAM （MESSAGE） BRING
　　YOU CORDIAL HOLIDAY GREETINGS AND OUR
　　SINCERE GOOD WISHES FOR YOUR PROSPER-
　　ITY AND HAPPINESS IN 19—

1. 致上耶誕問候。
2. 耶誕快樂，新年如意。
3. 願你耶誕，新年快樂（一切順利如意）。
4. 願耶誕帶給您快樂與幸福。
5. 謹祝耶誕快樂、幸福。
6. 祝耶誕愉快，新年快樂。
7. 在此聖誕佳節，恭祝平安、喜樂。

8. 願您聖誕平安，新年快樂。

9. 以我的赤誠祝賀您與家人聖誕快樂。

10. 願此祝賀，使您耶誕更加愉快。

11. 祝您聖誕快樂，新年如意。

12. 以我的愛祈願您，有個快樂的耶誕佳節及順利的新年。

13. 願聖誕的詳和、快樂在新的一年之中與你同在。

14. 願聖誕快樂，新年如意。

15. 在致耶誕問候的同時，甚是想念您，願您今天及來年皆快樂幸福。

16. 藉這封電報，衷心祝福耶誕快樂，並願您 19一年成功快樂。

6）祝客戶或同業新年快樂
（NEW YEAR GREETINGS）

實 例

1. MUCH LOVE AND BEST WISHES FOR A HAPPY NEW YEAR

2. MAY PEACE AND HAPPINESS BE YOURS IN THE NEW YEAR

3. MAY FORTUNE SMILE UPON YOU AND FAVOR YOU WITH MANY BLESSINGS

4. MAY THE COMING YEAR BRING YOU THE FULLEST MEASURE OF HEALTH AND HAPPINESS

5. MAY THE NEW YEAR BRING YOU HEALTH HAPPINESS AND ALL OTHER GOOD THINGS

6. SINCERELY HOPE THE NEW YEAR WILL HOLD FOR YOU A FULL MEASURE OF HEALTH AND HAPPINESS

7. I HOPE THE NEW YEAR WILL BRING YOU AND YOUR FAMILY EVERY HAPPINESS GOOD HEALTH AND CONTINUED SUCCESS

8. I SHALL BE GLAD IF THIS NEW YEARS LITTLE GREETING WILL ADD TO YOUR HAPPINESS AND PROSPERITY

1. 獻上我的愛與祝福，願您新年快樂。
2. 願您新年平安、快樂。
3. 願幸運之神對你微笑，並祝您更蒙護佑。
4. 願來年您身體健康，精神愉快。
5. 願新年帶給您健康、快樂以及其他許多的幸福。
6. 由衷祈求新的一年中您將十分地健康、快樂。
7. 希望新的一年帶給您一家人快樂、健康與順遂。
8. 希望新年的小小問候，能帶給您幸福與成功。

7) 向客戶或同業致同情與弔慰
(SYMPATHY AND CONDOLENCE)

實　例

1. HEARTFELT CONDOLENCE TO YOU
2. MY HEARTFELT SYMPATHY IN YOUR GREAT SORROW

3. MAY THE LORD BLESS AND SUSTAIN YOU IN
   YOUR LOSS
4. YOU HAVE MY HEARTFELT SYMPATHY IN THIS
   HOUR OF YOUR BEREAVEMENT
5. DEEPLY SHOCKED AND SADDENED TO LEARN
   OF （THE） SUDDEN PASSING OF YOUR WIFE
6. I AM GREATLY SHOCKED AT THE SAD NEWS
   YOU HAVE MY DEEPEST SYMPATHY
7. HEARTFELT CONDOLENCE TO YOU MAY YOU
   HAVE THE STRENGTH TO BEAR THIS GREAT
   AFFLICTION
8. SHOCKED TO LEARN OF YOUR MOTHERS （FA-
   THERS） DEATH I （WISH TO） EXPRESS
   （TO YOU） MY HEARTFELT CONDOLENCES
   IN YOUR AFFLICTION （BEREAVEMENT）
9. I HAVE JUST HEARD OF YOUR GREAT AF-
   FLICTION PLEASE ACCEPT MY HEARTFELT
   SYMPATHY
10. GREATLY GRIEVED AT （THE） SAD NEWS OF
    YOUR FATHERS （MOTHERS） DEATH WORDS
    FAIL TO EXPRESS MY DEEPEST SYMPATHY
11. PLEASE ACCEPT MY HEARTFELT （SINCERE）
    CONDOLENCE ON （THE） UNTIMELY DEATH
    OF PRESIDENT.... PLEASE CONVEY OUR
    PROFOUND SYMPATHY TO THE BEREAVED
    FAMILY

12. VERY SORRY TO HEAR （OF） YOUR ACCIDENT
    ALL （THE） STAFF JOINS ME （IN） EX-
    PRESSING SYMPATHY AND SINCERE WISHES
    FOR YOUR RAPID AND COMPLETE RECOVERY
13. DEEPLY PAINED TO HEAR OF THE FIRE
    （FLOOD） DAMAGE SUFFERED BY YOUR
    FACTORY AND HASTEN TO EXTEND OUR
    SINCERE SYMPATHY IF WE CAN ASSIST YOU
    IN ANY WAY PLEASE LET US KNOW

1. 由衷表示哀悼之意。
2. 我由衷同情您的深深的悲哀。
3. 願神保佑、扶持蒙受損失的您。
4. 在您傷慟之際，衷心表示我的哀悼。
5. 接到尊夫人突然過世的噩耗，真是萬分震驚與哀痛。
6. 我對噩耗非常震驚，謹致上我深深的同情之意。
7. 在此深致哀悼之意，希望你能承受此不幸。
8. 我對令堂（令尊）的仙逝表示哀悼,（謹向您）致上我的同情之意。
9. 我剛得知您的不幸遭遇，請接受我由衷的同情之意。
10. 聽到令尊（令堂）逝世的消息,不勝悲痛,言詞難表我最衷心的
    同情。
11. 對貴公司董事長溘然長逝的消息，謹表衷心哀悼之意…請向遺
    族表示我們深切的同情。
12. 聽到您發生意外，全體人員和我均感悲痛，謹表慰問之意並祝
    福您早日完全康復。
13. 聽到貴工廠遭到火（水）災的消息，非常痛心，匆此致上我們
    衷心同情之意。若有需要我們幫忙之處，願效犬馬之勞，請告知。

秘書必備常識

美國的 States 與 Dependencies 簡稱

Alabama	**AL**	Kentucky	**KY**
Alaska	**AK**	Louisiana	**LA**
Arizona	**AZ**	Maine	**ME**
Arkansas	**AR**	Maryland	**MD**
California	**CA**	Massachusetts	**MA**
Canal Zone	**CZ**	Michigan	**MI**
Colorado	**CO**	Minnesota	**MN**
Connecticut	**CT**	Mississippi	**MS**
Delaware	**DE**	Missouri	**MO**
District of		Montana	**MT**
Columbia	**DC**	Nebraska	**NE**
Florida	**FL**	Nevada	**NV**
Georgia	**GA**	New Hampshire	**NH**
Guam	**GU**	New Jersey	**NJ**
Hawaii	**HI**	New Mexico	**NM**
Idaho	**ID**	New York	**NY**
Illinois	**IL**	North Carolina	**NC**
Indiana	**IN**	North Dakota	**ND**
Iowa	**IA**	Ohio	**OH**
Kansas	**KS**	Oklahoma	**OK**

Oregon	**OR**	Utah	**UT**
Pennsylvania	**PA**	Vermont	**VT**
Puerto Rico	**PR**	Virginia	**VA**
Rhode Island	**RI**	Washington	**WA**
South Carolina	**SC**	West Virginia	**WV**
South Dakota	**SD**	Wisconsin	**WI**
Tennessee	**TN**	Wyoming	**WY**
Texas	**TX**		

加拿大的 Provinces 簡稱

Alberta	**AB**
British Columbia	**BC**
Labrador	**LB**
Manitoba	**MB**
New Brunswick	**NB**
Newfoundland	**NF**
Northwest Territories	**NT**
Nova Scotia	**NS**
Ontario	**ON**
Prince Edward Island	**PE**
Quebec	**PQ**
Saskatchewan	**SK**
Yukon Territory	**YT**

說英文高手 與傳統會話教材有何不同？

1. 我們學了那麼多年的英語會語，為什麼還不會說？

我們所使用的教材不對。傳統實況會話教材，如去郵局、在機場、看醫生等，勉強背下來，哪有機會使用？不使用就會忘記。等到有一天到了郵局，早就忘了你所學的。

2. 「說英文高手」這本書，和傳統的英語會話教材有何不同？

「說英文高手」這本書，以三句為一組，任何時候都可以說，可以對外國人說，也可以和中國人說，有時可自言自語說。例如：你幾乎天天都可以說：What a beautiful day it is! It's not too hot. It's not too cold. It's just right. 傳統的英語會話教材，都是以兩個人以上的對話為主，主角又是你，又是別人，當然記不下來。「說英文高手」的主角就是你，先從你天天可說的話開始。把你要說的話用英文表達出來，所以容易記下來。

3. 為什麼用「說英文高手」這本書，學了馬上就會說？

書中的教材，學起來有趣，一次說三句，不容易忘記。例如：你有很多機會可以對朋友說：Never give up. Never give in. Never say never.

4. 傳統會話教材目標不明確，一句句學，學了後面，忘了前面，一輩子記不起來。「說英文高手」目標明確，先從一次說三句開始，自我訓練以後，能夠隨時說六句以上，例如：你說的話，別人不相信，傳統會話只教你一句：I'm not kidding. 連這句話你都會忘掉。「說英文高手」教你一次說很多句：

I mean what I say.
I say what I mean.
I really mean it.

I'm not kidding you.
I'm not joking with you.
I'm telling you the truth.

你唸唸看，背這六句是不是比背一句容易呢？能夠一次說六句以上英文，你會有無比興奮的感覺，當說英文變成你的愛好的時候，你的目標就達成。

◉ 書180元 / 錄音帶四卷500元

✌ 「說英文高手」為劉毅老師最新創作，是學習出版公司轟動全國的暢銷新書。已被多所學校採用為會話教材。本書適合高中及大學使用，也適合自修。

全國最完整的文法書 ☆☆☆
文法寶典

▶ 劉 毅 編著

　　這是一套想學好英文的人必備的工具書,作者積多年豐富的敎學經驗,針對大家所不了解和最容易犯錯的地方,編寫成一套完整的文法書。

　　本書編排方式與衆不同,首先給讀者整體的槪念,再詳述文法中的細節部分,內容十分完整。文法說明以圖表爲中心,一目了然,並且務求深入淺出。無論您在考試中或其他書中所遇到的任何不了解的問題,或是您感到最煩惱的文法問題,查閱**文法寶典**均可迎刃而解。例如:哪些副詞可修飾名詞或代名詞?(P.228);什麼是介副詞?(P.543);那些名詞可以當副詞用?(P.100);倒裝句(P.629)、省略句(P.644)等特殊構句,爲什麼倒裝?爲什麼省略?原來的句子是什麼樣子?在**文法寶典**裏都有詳盡的說明。

　　例如,有人學了**觀念錯誤**的「假設法現在式」的公式,

> If + 現在式動詞……,主詞 + shall (will, may, can) + 原形動詞

只會造:If it rains, I will stay at home.

而不敢造:If you **are** right, I **am** wrong.

　　　　If I **said** that, I **was** mistaken.

　　　　(If 子句不一定用在假設法,也可表示條件子句的直說法。)

可見如果學文法不求徹底了解,反而成爲學習英文的絆腳石,對於這些易出錯的地方,我們都特別加以說明(詳見 P.356)。

　　文法寶典每册均附有練習,只要讀完本書、做完練習,您必定信心十足,大幅提高對英文的興趣與實力。

◉ 全套五册,售價**900**元。市面不售,請直接向本公司購買。

Editorial Staff

● **編譯** / 葉淑霞

● **校訂** / 劉　毅 · 劉文欽 · 史濟蘭 · 陳靜宜
　　　　　卓美玲 · 林叙儀 · 林慧馨

● **校閱** / Bruce S. Stewart · Kenyon T. Cotton
　　　　　David Brotman

● **美編** / 曹馨元 · 趙美惠 · 曹琇瑩

● **封面設計** / 曹馨元

● **打字** / 黃淑貞 · 賴秋燕 · 蘇淑玲 · 鄭梅芳

● **覆校** / 陳瑠琍 · 謝靜芳 · 蔡琇瑩 · 褚謙吉
　　　　　洪琴心 · 劉復苓

|||||||||||||| ● 學習出版公司門市部 ● ||||||||||||||||||

台北地區：台北市許昌街 10 號 2 樓 TEL：(02)2331-4060・2331-9209
台中地區：台中市綠川東街 32 號 8 樓 23 室
TEL：(04)223-2838

||||||||||||||||||||||||||||||||||||||||||||||||||||||||

最新秘書英語

編　　譯／葉　淑　霞
發　行　所／學習出版有限公司　　　　　☎ (02) 2704-5525
郵 撥 帳 號／0512727-2 學習出版社帳戶
登　記　證／局版台業 2179 號
印　刷　所／裕強彩色印刷有限公司
台 北 門 市／台北市許昌街 10 號 2 F　　　☎ (02) 2331-4060・2331-9209
台 中 門 市／台中市綠川東街 32 號 8 F 23 室　☎ (04) 223-2838
台灣總經銷／紅螞蟻圖書有限公司　　　　☎ (02) 2799-9490・2657-0132
美國總經銷／Evergreen Book Store　　☎ (818) 2813622

售價：新台幣二百二十元正
2000 年 10 月 1 日一版六刷